ISBN: 978-1-4759-3308-6 (sc)
ISBN: 978-1-4759-3309-3 (e)

Printed in the United States of America

iUniverse rev. date: 10/03/2013

Registration No: 1094673 (Registration of Copyright in Canada)

I Mar

Michele Ketzmerick

iUniverse LLC
Bloomington

Contents

Acknowledgments

I am grateful to my husband Murray for his patience throughout this process. He provided much feedback, especially as I desperately tried to avoid offending anyone while writing about such a sensitive and controversial subject. He encouraged me to forge ahead and insisted that if I was going to start a project, that I ought to finish it, and it must be done properly.

I am grateful as well, that I found an editor who helped me to do just that. With much proficiency and patience Joan Dixon pushed me toward competence, to express my thoughts more clearly and in a more organized way. Being a first time writer, I appreciated that she shared feedback and suggestions clearly and always in a gentle manner.

My children Devin, Kara, and Ty shared their interest in my writing probably long after the feeling had faded. Their capacity for critical thinking keeps me humble and I am proud beyond measure of the integrity and character that they each possess.

The beautiful picture on the front cover, taken by Murray, was the view from our villa in St. Lucia in February 2012.

Introduction

I grew up a part of the "One True Church," convinced I would be the fortunate recipient of an afterlife in heaven. As I got older and began to learn more about my religion—through the journey that I outline in this book—I encountered difficulty in digging out from under all the dogma and indoctrination. I discovered a dark side to religion making us afraid to speak up, afraid of the consequences of asking questions about things that may have made sense 2,000 years ago, but possibly no longer today. Despite the fear and guilt I felt for doubting the beliefs of my family and community, I finally took the leap and sought answers to forbidden questions.

After decades of identifying as Roman Catholic, I finally understood what having blind faith *really* meant. I started to write (in a journal at first) when I began critically thinking about the belief system of my childhood. The more I read and wrote, the more I considered compiling my insights into a book. I believed others might be interested.

For the non-religious who choose to read my subjective stories and insights, you might think as my husband did: "I don't see the big deal. I wasn't brought up with that." At the other end of the spectrum—if you have a strong faith—there may be no room in your own mind to consider similar questions or to admit that parts of religion may no longer make sense to you.

When I decided that I could not merely accept the things that I had been told, I found, fortunately, other people who had similar questions, people whose inquiring minds were no longer content with unsatisfying responses from the Church and its leaders of men who claim to know the mind of God. I learned through the process that nonbelievers are not the monsters I was taught to believe they were: without a belief in a god or gods, people can still value reason, kindness, and compassion. Ironically, I married someone who had never been religious, but it took me almost sixteen years of marriage to understand what that really meant. Despite his secular nature, my husband has always been supportive and never suggested that my religiosity was peculiar in any way. He always maintained that if faith in God was important to me, then it was fine with him, believable or not. I am grateful for his respect and the space that allowed the sometimes strange, but always interesting, journey you'll read about in the following pages.

This is a time when more people, especially young people, are asking questions about belief systems that no longer seem relevant to their lives. This is a generation that likely will be less influenced by archaic books written by men in the Bronze Age. As I learned about many other belief systems and enjoyed the surprises of a world outside of faith and organized religion, I had to ultimately decide what I should, or could, leave behind.

> *Men become civilized, not in proportion to their willingness to believe, but in proportion to their readiness to doubt.*—H. L. Mencken

Chapter 1

I Want to be a Nun

And this I believe: that the free, exploring mind of the individual human is the most valuable thing in the world.—John Steinbeck, *East of Eden*

As was normal in our area of the country, I grew up going to church on Sundays. This always prompted commotion in our house, as there were chores to complete and nine of us to get ready and on the road to town. All of us were resistant to going, except the one brother out of my six siblings who I knew (with pride) would be a priest someday.

Every Sunday it was the same routine. In our Catholic Church, there was no Sunday school so we all had to sit through the service without talking or moving except to sit or kneel or stand when prompted. Our family took up an entire pew in the church and when Dad would fall asleep at one end of the row, Mom would pass the message along to nudge him awake at the other end of the pew. He would startle awake, usually not quietly. My brothers became altar servers eventually, but I was not allowed because I was a girl. I didn't understand why only the boys got to wear the white cotton puffy-sleeved dresses. Eventually I became

1

more involved in the church as well; I participated in the readings and played the guitar. I enjoyed helping the nuns when it was time to decorate the church for each celebration of a new season, especially at Christmas and Easter. They were so good with crafts and decorations, which I couldn't help but admire, and I began visiting them at the convent regularly. No matter what time of day, a smell of homemade soup permeated from the convent's otherwise sterile walls. I associated the vivid aroma with kindness, gentleness and peace.

Most of the nuns were teachers at our Catholic School, referred to as the "Separate School" and one of my favourites, my grade three teacher, especially exuded peace and kindness. I remember running to meet her at the caragana shrubs at the edge of the school yard just to ensure that I could walk next to her as she returned from the convent after lunch. I was always amazed at how white and clean her skin was. When I visited her after school, I eagerly anticipated her retrieving a snack from the kitchen just for me. I even tried on a veil one day, imagining the nun's life for me.

A few years later, my grade five teacher also treated me like I was special. I asked her one day how she knew that she was supposed to be a nun. She explained that she could hear the unmistakable voice in her heart. She said that there was never any doubt for her. As much as I quietly listened and prayed for it, I never did hear any voices, in my heart or otherwise. Eventually I accepted that as much as I liked hanging around the convent, the smell of homemade soup and the loving women who called the convent home, I probably wasn't meant to live my life as a nun.

There seemed to be something so special about these women—a peacefulness and a certainty of their purpose. I remember wondering why they had been chosen and not me, but thought maybe the call would come later in my life. I continued to attend Sunday mass regularly, where the Bible was considered sacred, and unquestioningly the "Word of God." I also attended Christian Ethics, a mandatory religion class for Catholic students. At that time, religion, like the nuns, meant comfort, love, and peace to me.

Religion was infused into my daily life as well. I was terrified of thunderstorms. I hated the violent loud cracking of thunder and what I assumed was the imminent threat of electrocution from the lightning. As a young girl, I would strain to reach up to each window pane in our house with the jar of holy water. (Holy water is just tap water that has been turned into holy water as the result of a priest saying a prayer over it.) We always had some on hand in case it would be needed. I don't remember anyone else in the family ever using it, but I had one especially important use for this very special liquid. Carefully, with complete faith in its efficacy, I dipped my finger in the jar and made a cross on each window. My brothers laughed at me but I believed that was a minor consequence for doing my part to keep us all safe.

I spoke about religion from time to time at home, particularly with the brother that I thought would be a priest. We discussed whether all the stories and miracles could be true. After going back and forth, we always came to the same cautious conclusion: we were better off to play it safe and believe—just in case. If it wasn't true then we lost nothing. If we didn't believe and it was true, we would surely go to hell. An afterlife of never-ending torment was just too much of a risk to take. I didn't realize at the time that this was not *really* believing, at least not in an honest way. (Incidentally, he never did become a priest.)

It had to be true, I concluded as a young girl. Why would the kind, honest nuns lie to us; why would our parents go through the hassle of forcing us to go to church every Sunday? And really, if it was good enough for our mom and dad to believe in, it was good enough for us. I told myself that they surely wouldn't deceive us, not on purpose anyway.

I grew up feeling quite relieved that I was Catholic. Thanks to my parents and being born where I was born, I belonged to the "best" religion, the One True Faith, called so because it offered the only real way to heaven. I remember feeling sorry for the public school kids across the road because they did not have any idea what they were missing and worse, what they and their families were in for after they died. They were unfortunate lost souls who did not even know it. Unlike us, they did not have priests or nuns to be nice to them and guide them. The public school kids also seemed a little scary and unpredictable to me—how did they know what was right and wrong without religion class and Catholic sermons every Sunday? In my child's mind, I worried: without "proper" guidance from our holy book or holy people to tell them how to live, could they, would they, be violent at any moment?

More worrisome for me were my non-church-attending cousins whom I loved so much but who would unfortunately not meet me in heaven. I believed in heaven for the faithful so it followed that hell would be the alternative for non-believers. I wasn't sure about the Protestants but it seemed to me in those early years that any chance of heaven for them was slim. It was as if they practiced "religion-lite" or something less. They didn't have the sacraments, including confession and confirmation, to save them from an almost certain eternity in hell. I didn't like thinking about loved ones being tortured for an eternity, but I could fall asleep reassuring myself that at least I wouldn't be one of them—thanks to belonging to the One True Church.

My home was similar to many others of that time, comprised of a large family, busy parents, lots of stress and chaos and, understandably, little time for nurturing. There was little money and lots of work on a dairy farm. We were happy to be fed, clothed and allowed to enjoy ball tournaments in the summer and hockey in the winter. On hot summer days, we dreaded weeding the large garden, but enjoyed the trips to a nearby lake to swim once the work was completed. I did well in school and kept busy with most of the same activities as my brothers, achieving self-esteem through many sport accomplishments. We had the things necessary for contentment and survival.

As I grew out of a relatively normal childhood and into the teenage years, temptations grew and the more that I would seek out love and acceptance, the more I would get into trouble. Poor choices, guilt and fear soon became common themes in my life. I was barely a teenager when I wrote in my journal, that I had a boyfriend for the first time. He had kissed me during a hockey game. There was a group of us who would leave the game and hide in one of the rodeo grounds food booths just outside the skating rink. It was so exciting! I soon realized it was not my calling to be a nun. I had discovered boys!

When I discovered the most "sinful" intimacy later in high school, however, my guilt was profound. I knew then that it would be necessary to take advantage of the forgiveness offered through the confessional. Eventually, as temptations increased in those days, and especially as the fear of death and hell overwhelmed me, I stayed close to the dark wooden closet of the confessional, with the reassurance that I could be forgiven, no matter how grave the transgression.

It wasn't until I attended a class called Religions of the World in university that I first thought about other beliefs, and considered that other major religions might have some validity. The Hindus, the Buddhists, the Islamists, and the Jews around the world all seemed to spend more time and energy devoted to their faith. Their adherence to their respective religious practices seemed to indicate a devoutness that seemed greater, and perhaps more meaningful, than the religion that I grew up with. The questions in my mind at the time included: How could such devout religious people be wrong in their beliefs? How could such faithful people go to hell? How can we be sure that Catholics are the only true faithful? What if I happened to be in the wrong religion?

At that time I wasn't ready to look any further into why I believed what I believed, or why I stuck with the original plan, but I remember feeling some guilt for the questions that surfaced. I reminded myself to have faith in what I had learned in Christian Ethics and continue to be grateful for the *luck of the draw*—of being born into the One True Faith.

Then a crisis forced me to challenge the beliefs of a lifetime and to face the true origin of an irrational fear of death. Before I shut down almost completely, I found out that this was not the way that I wanted to live or die.

Chapter 2

Contemplating Death

Question with boldness even the existence of God; because if there be one, he must more approve of the homage of reason than that of blindfolded fear.—Thomas Jefferson

I have started and stopped writing this account several times over the past few years, overwhelmed with learning facts and ideas that contradicted beliefs that I grew up with. Then I would start again when I read about things that I believed were too important not to question or research further. I buried my nose in books and strained my eyes reading mounds of interesting material that would normally have been off limits in a Catholic perspective. I wasn't trying to be defiant or rebellious and I was confident it wasn't just a phase. I wanted to understand why I believed what I believed. Just declaring that I was a person of faith was no longer enough for me.

I started to research many things that I had once believed to be true. The belief systems taught at school had been reinforced at church. As children, we had trusted our parents, our teachers, our churches, and our communities to guide and direct us. But as an adult, I felt more compelled to question the status quo and what it all really meant. Cracks developed in the foundation of my faith. I started to question things that I had taken for granted as true as a child, that no longer made sense: a talking snake, a virgin birth, human sacrifice and a resurrection, to name just a few extraordinary ideas. Thinking critically about it all had never been an option until I faced one significant incident.

The Catholic Catalyst

I was young, still in my early forties, and had been active all of my life so felt I was in relatively decent physical shape. Slowly though, I had been feeling my body betray me. One autumn, the pain in my back worsened to a near debilitating degree. I was frustrated not being able to function normally. It was difficult to get up to go to work each day because of lack of sleep due to excruciating pain. At six o'clock in the morning, I would finally drift off due to exhaustion and wake to the alarm soon after. I thought to myself, this is it: life as I know it is over. Although I'd had some back problems over the years, there was never anything seriously wrong that could not be fixed by a trip to the chiropractor and regular massage therapy. Now, however, I was also experiencing problems with my right foot, and some vision issues, and I needed assistance to put on my socks.

Despite the usual remedies, the pain just kept getting worse. With the addition of more symptoms there was concern of a neurological problem. Fortunately, some of the more serious illnesses such as Multiple Sclerosis and Parkinson's disease were ruled out early on. The idea that the pain and other symptoms were all in my head crept in from time to time, especially as more tests were done without any conclusive diagnosis. Maybe the inevitable was finally happening—I was losing my mind! I joked with my family that it had been only a matter of time, as we all expected.

My physician was doing his best to find out what was wrong through CT scans and wait-listing me for an MRI. The symptom of worsening night pain was of such concern that I was referred for a bone scan to rule out bone cancer. On the day of the scan, my husband and I drove ninety minutes to the city for the appointment. Sitting in the waiting room caused increasing feelings of despair, especially after I visited with a former co-worker who was dying rapidly from bone cancer. Finally my name was called. With thoughts of something equally serious and terminal going through my mind, I felt the technician loosely bind my feet to ensure I was in the proper position and then I was told to lay as still as possible for an hour. When the scan was finished and read by a physician, the technician returned to where I was waiting in the scan room to tell me I would have to wait a while. They needed a second scan.

Of course the worst-case scenario raced through my mind. Throughout the hour of the next scan, I thought about my three kids, my husband, my extended family, and imagined the worst. How could I ever tell my kids such horrible news; how would my husband Murray cope and start over? I tried to stop myself from thinking about this, but with little success. Finally I tried to relax, telling myself that it was just a test and the results, like the others, would be negative. But, the dark worry of dying young would not let go.

When the technician finished, I tried everything to convince him to tell me the results, so that I wouldn't have to wait for days more. I was desperately wishing for even a hint that all was okay. Fine, I pleaded, leave the bad news and the details to the doctor in later days, but allow at least some relief in the interim, for God's sake! Even though I understood the reason, much to my disappointment, he remained professional and followed proper protocol.

On the trip home, I was in a trance. For ninety minutes I was unable to even begin to talk about the paralyzing fear that I was going to die. I had read that bone cancer was neither gentle nor lengthy—an excruciatingly painful death. My husband tried to talk with me but I was too consumed with imagining the worst, and every detail of it. I was catastrophizing and I knew it, but I was too overwhelmed to infuse any positive thoughts into the depressing and irrational ones. I was forced by this circumstance to think seriously about my untimely demise. The world had stopped for me.

That night, and early into the next morning, I planned my funeral. I thought about how I would tell each of my kids. Should we all be together; should I tell them separately? I thought about their weddings and their futures without me. I thought about my mom and dad and how devastated they would be at losing their only daughter. I didn't want them to go through the horrific pain of outliving one of their children.

I cried most of that night and between sobs, shared my thoughts with my husband. He held me as I contemplated the end of my life. It might sound overly dramatic but this was the first time that I had ever thought about my own death in such an inevitable and serious way. For several days, my mortality remained at the forefront of my thoughts. The fear of death had shaken me to my core.

As I made attempts to move my thoughts beyond death, I reminded myself that I had been baptized and was up to date on the required sacraments. Catholics believed that, thanks to Jesus, a life in the hereafter follows death on earth. But even in that promise, I did not find comfort. I could not imagine the end of me. What if—as my brother and I had contemplated as children—this life on earth is all there is? After all my life's ups and downs were considered, what if I hadn't followed the rules as I should have?

*   *   *

Despite the difficulty of maintaining my usual routine, I forced myself to get up and go to work during this horribly long week. My responsibilities hadn't stopped and I knew that I needed to keep busy to maintain some level of sanity while I awaited the news.

I was in the middle of a board meeting when my cell phone lit up and I recognized my family physician's phone number. My heart was beating rapidly as I excused myself to hear my doctor explain that he wanted to call as soon as he received the results. I took a deep breath in as he shared the news: the bone scan was negative. A huge weight was lifted and I could breathe out again! Eventually I found out that the diagnosis was not nearly as dramatic as my response to the tests had been. The *good* news: my spine had been degenerating due to sports injuries and some serious falls, and I could expect continued pain and degeneration as I aged. I also had some residual effects of a concussion suffered one year earlier. But, as far as I knew on that day, I was not going to die anytime soon. I do not remember ever being so happy and grateful to be alive. I floated for days.

Several days later though, the thought occurred to me . . . for someone with a supposedly sturdy faith, why had I been so terrified of death, of heaven, of being with God? That just did not make sense. Perhaps my faith wasn't so strong after all—but if not, why not? I had grown up Catholic, went to confession (a lot) and went to church as an adult—at least for weddings, funerals, and important holidays. Being a person of faith, why was I so terrified about the end of my life? Leaving loved ones, especially children, was part of it, but then, like the stadium lights exploding on in the darkness, the reason occurred to me. I had made some significant mistakes in my life; what if some were inexcusable, or too big to push through the absolution loophole? Moreover, what if my Catholicism was not the true religion? What if I was not heaven-bound after all? What if my *hereafter* was going to be *hell forever*? Oh my God! I thought. Hell is what I feared most! Not just the idea of hell, but all the horrific details: gnashing teeth, burning flesh and eternal screaming in pain.

There had been times in my life when I could have made better choices. I thought back to the pain that I had caused my children, particularly when my former husband and I divorced, and the relationships that I'd regretted during the following tumultuous years. Even with two wonderful young children at home, I had never felt adequate without a partner reinforcing that I was loved. I thought about each time my decisions had hurt someone and felt profound shame. How could I now be sure of a clean slate after the many transgressions for which I had sought absolution from a priest? The more I thought about it, the more uncertain I became that I would be going to heaven. I felt tormented by my own past and deathly afraid when I contemplated the end of it. This fear was irrational and contradictory to faith. To make things worse, the lack of faith itself was sinful.

I became determined to make some sense of the confusion. Maybe hell wasn't real after all? Maybe I just wanted it to be a myth because I was afraid of the possibility that I deserved to go there. But, how could a loving God hold this everlasting torture over his beloved children? There was nothing that I could think of that would warrant such an end for my own children. Hell did not make sense to me as a Catholic, or as a parent.

Was my faith faltering? Was I finished believing without questioning? I was determined to understand this fear that was such a debilitating, undercurrent in my life. I had been taught to believe that when we die, we'd be with Jesus in heaven. Now, if I was *really* convinced of that, it would follow that I should be at least a little less afraid of the end of my earthly life.

So, as scary as it was, I started reading about the big fiery elephant in the room, hell. If there was even a slim chance that I would be going there, then I wanted to learn more about it. It was sort of like doing the research on resorts in the Caribbean before booking a trip: I wanted to be prepared for the destination, but first to find out if it was in fact an actual destination.

The Bible seemed like a good resource to begin with. I had read it cover-to-cover through religion classes in high school but from it remembered mostly God's love and the celebration of the sacraments. Reading it again, I found the usual nasty descriptions of hell but more interesting, I discovered that the most insignificant actions, even thoughts, could send us there and that many of these ticket-to-hell items did not make sense.

*The Son of man shall send forth his angels, and they
shall gather out of his kingdom all things that offend,
and them which do iniquity; And shall cast them into
a furnace of fire: there shall be wailing and gnashing
of teeth.* Matthew 13:41-42

*If thy hand or thy foot offend thee, cut them off, and
cast them from thee: it is better for thee to enter into
life halt or maimed, rather than having two hands
or two feet to be cast into everlasting fire.* Matthew
18:8-9

*Then said the king to the servants, Bind him hand
and foot, and take him away, and cast him into
outer darkness, there shall be weeping and gnashing
of teeth.* Matthew 22:13

*. . . into hell, into the fire that never shall be
quenched. Where their worm dieth not, and the fire
is not quenched.* Mark 9:43-48

*. . . And he cried and said, Father Abraham, have
mercy on me, and send Lazarus, that he may dip the
tip of his finger in water, and cool my tongue; for I
am tormented in this flame.* Luke 16:23

*The hour is coming, in which all that are in the
graves shall hear his voice, and shall come forth; they
that have done good, unto the resurrection of life;
and they that have done evil, unto the resurrection of
damnation.* John 5:28-29

> *In flaming fire taking vengeance on them that know not God, and that obey not the gospel of our Lord Jesus Christ: Who shall be punished with everlasting destruction.* 2 Thessalonians 1:8-9

> *The same shall drink of the wine of the wrath of God, which is poured out without mixture into the cup of his indignation; and he shall be tormented with fire and brimstone in the presence of the holy angels, and in the presence of the Lamb.* Revelation 14:10-11

And those were just a few examples! None of this looked "loving" to me. I reminded myself that Catholics believe that Jesus died for our sins—all sins—when he died on the cross. I felt grateful for this, especially in my state of self-loathing due to so many years of engrained guilt. But, since I was not dying any time soon, I decided that I had the time to keep researching the place that, in the deepest part of me, I had spent a lifetime fearing.

Death for Catholics

Although I had tried to live a decent life, I believed that there was still the possibility that I would not end up in heaven. Imagine burning for an eternity in darkness! I thought about hell when I was young, worried that I could be judged and sent there. Joking with one of my brothers on the way home from school one day, we were discussing the rules of our religion and were a bit concerned about going to hell on a technicality. What if we had committed a sin without realizing that it was a sin? We thought we had an "out" with confession, but would it actually work? We decided in the end to not take the chance, and that we had nothing to lose by believing. Looking back on that time, I now believe that there had been a lot to lose. I lived in fear of this place.

After doing some research on the origins of hell and Satan, I was shocked and embarrassed. These concepts had been invented by humans. Hell had never been "discovered" as an actual place and captured on video for us! It had merely served as a brilliant way to *encourage* the masses of uneducated people on earth at that time to believe what was said and written, or face the horrific consequences described. The Church had made up a story that continues to scare the *hell* out of everyone.

The rest is truly history: most people did fall in line, listened to, and believed the wise elders of the tribes. Who would want to take the risk of spending eternity with never-ending suffering? This great "story" continues to work today as the threat is held over our children in devout families and in faith schools.

I really was not prepared for what I found out when I began to more closely consider hell and other beliefs. I learned that humans, regardless of lack of proof or scientific evidence, will and do believe almost anything. I did. It does not matter if these things are true or not. The only thing that does matter seems to be whether the belief in some sort of father figure in the sky could bring comfort and provide hope in an eventual afterlife with him in heaven. And, the promises come in all shapes and sizes depending on the religion. Santa's nice and naughty list comes to mind, but it changes depending on the religion.

I thought back to the softer Catholic teachings from school—the more pleasant content about love and peace. We had learned about the existence of hell but it had not been the main focus, unlike the more intense doctrine of fire and brimstone in other religions. Perhaps this is because Catholics seem less reliant on the Bible than other Christian religions that I have read about. The fact that I carried the fear of hell throughout the first four decades of my life, however, was an indication that even subtle indoctrination was profoundly effective.

A little voice in the back of my mind kept reminding me that although I was asking questions, salvation might still be available to me. There was a chance that my soul could be saved. But there were also times when I would think about parts of my life, especially what I refer to as the "black years" of stumbling around trying to move forward, that provoked uncertainty about whether my behaviour would warrant the afterlife that I was trying to avoid.

What not to do if you wanted to get to heaven? Premarital sex, divorce, and death by suicide: I had some lingering questions about each of these "sins."

Chapter 3

Being Catholic

I have always felt that doubt was the beginning of wisdom, and the fear of God was the end of wisdom.—Clarence Darrow, famous American lawyer and writer

This chapter was the most difficult for me to write because Catholicism is the religion of my family. Early on, even though I would continue to self-identify as Roman Catholic on census and medical forms, I was slowly feeling my Catholic self eroding. But, I still had feelings of regret as I began to identify more with non-believers than with being Catholic. My intention was not to be hurtful, disrespectful or intolerant and I hope that whoever might choose to read this will regard my experiences with an open mind and heart.

I had more intriguing sources than I needed and for months the books and journal entries just sat in a pile on the floor beside my bed. There was enough information for a book of my own, but because of the sensitive nature of the subject, I struggled to begin the daunting task of organizing it all. Unlike any other ideology, religion is generally off limits to criticism or questioning, and it was definitely not acceptable to discuss its absurdities. The digging I was doing was certainly forbidden—and I found out why.

It all started benignly. I had grown up proudly Catholic, usually following most of the rules, but eventually attending mass began to feel like a chore. By the time I graduated from high school, I was attending services only for funerals or weddings. Even though my church attendance and degree of faith greatly fluctuated as I married and had children, I realized now that I did not know the actual rules of the Catholic Church. I realized also, that I had followed along like a sheep most of my life, without really knowing why. Despite the guilt that I felt about it, I made a conscious decision to start asking questions. What were the rules of my faith? Since I didn't know why I remained Catholic after childhood, I didn't know why I should choose to continue to be Catholic in my forties. What did being Catholic really mean? I had to find some answers to these serious questions.

The things that I always liked about church included the smell of incense, the architecture of the cathedrals, the pancake breakfasts and the music. I loved Christian music and I enjoyed playing the guitar in church while I was growing up. What I failed to realize, until I visited other churches, was how much more wonderful the music could be when the congregation really sings along. I was usually frustrated as I looked around at the quiet congregation, amazed at how little volume came out of a large church even half full of people. This was hardly rejoicing! My mom told me, "Well the church isn't there to entertain us!" Well that's a relief, I thought, because I sure wasn't entertained. Nor was I inspired.

I decided to re-read the Holy Book, the inspired "Word of God." First I wanted to take a closer look at original sin. What does it really mean? Thomas Aquinas explained it this way: *"Accordingly the original sin of all men was in Adam indeed, as in its principal cause, according to the words of the Apostle (Romans 5:12): "In whom all have sinned": whereas it is in the bodily semen, as in its instrumental cause, since it is by the active power of the semen that original sin together with human nature is transmitted to the child . . ."*[1]

Oh dear, I never really thought about it like this. I had never really thought about it all! I just believed the teachers, the nuns and the priests who had taught us that Eve had been the primary problem when she convinced Adam to eat the apple, the forbidden fruit. They didn't mention the details of bodily semen transmission and of the actual sinful nature with which we exit the womb. At Easter we had felt compassion for Jesus' suffering but had been more excited by Easter Sunday when we remembered that he rose again to prove what God promised—that our sins, including this one we were born with, could be forgiven. It had all made perfect sense for decades. I had thanked God many times for providing a way to heaven despite my innate sinful nature. But, now I thought, can we really have our sins "thrown onto" someone else (Jesus) without it affecting our sense of responsibility? I considered the innocent baby—how can he or she be damaged or sinful? How could I have sinned before I was even born?

I began to understand the question I'd recently heard about whether Adam and Eve really existed. Had they really

---

[1]   *The Catholic Route to Birth Control,* accessed on April 14, 2012, http://www.orthodoxchristianity.net/forum/index.php?topic=29748.195;wap2,

been put on the earth to begin populating the world? It takes only basic high school biology to figure out that this would not have been possible scientifically, but the implications of calling it a myth were immense. Without Adam and Eve, there would be no 'fall' of mankind from grace. Without the fall, there would be no need for redemption and then of course the church would lose this "original sin" and its power over the actions of the people.

It also occurred to me that Catholics not only believe in original sin but also in human torture and sacrifice. I had to question this other core belief of the Catholic faith: the story of Jesus dying on the cross. Jesus' father basically sent him on a suicide mission to pay vicariously for future wrongdoings of humankind. Jesus died on the cross to wipe the slate clean, to atone for original sin and open the way for heaven. My personal philosophy has always been that I should take responsibility for my own bad decisions and yet, for decades, I had also been convinced that this free pass for sinners was a truly great idea (though not for Jesus of course). I always felt such a relief at least for a day or two after confession because I knew that if I was struck by a car after absolution, I would almost certainly go to heaven. The rest of the time though, I lived in fear—of a God I was also supposed to love.

In the Easter story, I had always felt sorry for Judas because of how he had been mistreated for giving Jesus up to the Roman soldiers. Many biblical translations include his suicidal death by hanging. Judas should really have been our hero. What if no one had given him up? Jesus would not have been captured by the Romans and then the resurrection would not have happened. How could my sins have ever been forgiven? I wondered why no one else had thought this through. Also, as a result of this story, an entire race, the Jews, had been blamed for Jesus' death and the Catholic Church has only recently exonerated them. If this was all part of God's plan, why blame mortal humans for being the pawns in the divine plan? According to the story then, without Judas and the Jews, the resurrection would not have been possible!

I kept asking myself, why would a father demonstrate his love for his son by subjecting him to torture to save us from ourselves, especially when he created us sinful to begin with? It was sounding more and more like nonsense. Comedian Julia Sweeney puts the suffering of Jesus in perspective in her show, *Letting Go of God;* "Jesus really just had a bad weekend." And, he didn't really die! Maybe we could compare his suffering with those of the women who were burned alive during the Inquisition, by people who believed that they were also doing what God required of them. Or, compare it to a loved one's excruciatingly, painful struggle with cancer, or any other serious illness.

For a long time, I had believed in the intercession by apostles and priests, that it was actually through human sacrifice that our sins were forgiven, and that the priest somehow turned wine into the actual blood of Jesus and crackers into his body, literally wine to blood, bread to flesh. I never questioned it but still judged other belief systems for some of their own absurd practices and beliefs: reincarnation and the multiple gods of Hinduism, the overt oppression of women in Islam on behalf of their ancient holy book, the weird extraterrestrial component of Scientology, the magic underwear of the Mormons, the strict Sabbath rules of Judaism, and the belief in the inerrancy of the Bible for fundamentalist Christians, to mention a few.

It became difficult to find credibility in a belief system that seemed to be changing even some of its basic tenets. In

1999 I heard the news that the Catholic Pope, John Paul II, had finally declared that heaven, hell and purgatory were not actual places but states of being on earth. He described hell as a state that we create for ourselves on earth when we make choices that lead us further from God. The discounting of Adam and Eve, heaven and hell, and later, the concept of limbo, by a pope were significant changes. The fundamental belief in limbo—without baptism, babies stayed in a sort of never-never land, with no chance of ever going to heaven—held by Catholics for centuries, had further devastated young parents mourning the deaths of their babies. Limbo was overturned by Pope Benedict in an approved report by the International Theological Commission in April 2007.

Purgatory (a "holding area" for people to be prepared or purified before they were considered for heaven) is another concept in the Catholic Church that is nowhere to be found in the Bible. It holds strong for good reason because people like to believe that with prayers and masses said for the departed—for a fee—the soul of a loved one will more likely (and more quickly) move along to heaven. Who wouldn't want to help a loved one in this way? How could any person risk *not* doing it? What a small price to expedite a critical process. The idea of these "indulgences" turned into a lucrative business of course. It has been said that the Vatican was built on these paid prayers to God. And I remember hearing a motto used to describe the Catholic Church—pray, pay, obey. But, I wondered, why would God need the money? To be fair, money is not the only type of indulgence. Building churches, donating to hospitals, or organizing crusades were also considered good works that would be rewarded by God.[2]

I had also never questioned the unnatural celibacy of priests and why that practice had come into being but I more recently tried to find a satisfactory answer to why only males could be priests or leaders of the Church. What I found during the course of my research was not an answer but perhaps a side effect, on which I focus in the next chapter.

I once believed that outside my church, there could be no salvation—that Catholics were the only owners of the truth. I had also learned from a young age that the words of church leaders were to be trusted without question. It is no wonder that we are discouraged from asking questions, considering what I found when I started looking. I had trusted the church leaders, the priests, to tell me what to do but that practice reduced my need to think for myself. I was told to just believe and trust that priests know the mind of God. Yet, as one of his children, why could I not hear him directly? Was an intercessor really necessary?

There were specific subjects wherein the rules were quite clear, and where there was plenty of advice to be had. I was starting to see the religious irrationality behind the Catholic view of many other issues, especially regarding these "sinful" big three—sex, divorce, and suicide.

---

[2]   *Indulgences*, Catholic Encyclopedia, accessed April 14, 2012. http://www.newadvent.org/cathen/07783a.htm

The Catholic Obsession with Sex

I am beginning the "sin list" with sex for a few reasons. First, it was the first of many Catholic rules that I was conflicted about, and second, because I can. I can finally talk about sex without feeling ashamed of myself, my body and its primal life force. Intimacy was the first hint of a significant inner struggle with my religious upbringing.

I became conflicted because sex was something that seemed to be so natural. I had grown up on a farm with chickens, pigs and cows so we were surrounded by nature and natural tendencies. I remember once trying to kick the rooster off the hen because I had thought they were fighting. The boar was not so lucky, as I had a shovel in my hands when nature was attempting to take its course. In my naiveté I was just trying to protect the girls from what seemed like a vicious unprovoked attack. As farm kids, though, we probably found out sooner than urban kids how babies were made.

When I was dating in high school, there had been the usual pressure to have sex, especially in serious relationships. Affection was natural, the feelings were natural and I was very curious about what all the fuss was. Why was something so natural so forbidden? Of course, eventually I chose to satisfy this curiosity. There was immediate intense regret—not because it was a horrible experience but because of the guilt—I knew I had committed the worst premarital sin. How was I going to tell the priest about something so intimate? But I had to tell him because I deduced that confessing would be much less uncomfortable than spending an eternity in hell.

It was humiliating to say it out loud to someone, especially a holy man, a man of God, but the relief that

I felt was amazing! I must admit that looking back, it was also a little creepy. Each time (it may have happened more than once) I was absolved. I was so grateful that God would forgive this horrible sinner and even more grateful that I could start over. Well, I enjoyed starting over and over and over. The list of *Our Fathers* and *Hail Marys* lengthened with each trip to the confessional.

I moved away after high school but continued to go to church once in a while, mostly because I felt too guilty not to, and because I loved the music, the incense, and it still seemed important to at least keep one foot in the door of the One True Church. On return trips home from college, I started dating someone new to the community. We fell in love and things progressed as they had in previous serious relationships. I had thought that it might be worth trying to abstain until marriage but the good intention was not long lived. I was back in confession more times than I would like to admit. Finally I proposed to him so that we could get married and I could stop sinning and wasting the priest's time. I did love him, but the sense of urgency to marry was strong. I wanted to be pious like other Catholic women that I knew. The prospect of hell, as irrational as it was, remained in the back of my mind, so I got married when I was only 20.

The message in the Catholic Church continues to be abstinence before marriage. Well, I hadn't quite made it and I suspect that there are at least a few other Catholics who hadn't. It is a rule that began with male church leaders, a rule that turned sex into an embarrassment, a shameful, sinful act. The aging virgin male leaders of the Church continue to tell us what to do with our bodies—when we can have sex, how we can have sex, and with whom. Did they expect orgies in the streets without these rules? As I read more about Catholic history and teaching, I learned about the origin of the shame of sex, and the importance of the repression of sex. Through its rules about homosexuality and gay marriage, the unnatural celibacy of priests and nuns, its rather ridiculous rules regarding masturbation and sex before marriage, and the ironic lack of a moral response to the rampant priestly pedophilia, the Church has proved that it has used sex as just another form of control. The more I read, the more I recognized that the Catholic Church is obsessed with sex.

Finally, I made my intimate life none of the Church's business and am no longer ashamed.

Suicide for Catholics

I was taught that suicide was a sin, one of the most grave, a sin with no hope for redemption. How could suicide be considered one of the worst sins, especially when an underlying influence can be mental illness? I had to ask, where is the compassion of God in this? If you believe in God as a parent, how could you believe that he could send anyone, after a lifetime of suffering with a debilitating mental illness such as depression, to an eternity of further torment? It sounded ridiculous when I thought about it.

People who choose to take their own life often see no other way out of their desperate struggle. This may be their last attempt to stop the pain; they have given up. This warrants our compassion and our love, not our judgment or God's judgment.

If we think it through, many of us are committing suicide daily, but in a more subtle way; we're killing ourselves sooner than necessary when we eat unhealthy food, avoid dealing with stress in a healthy way, have negative attitudes, smoke, and drink too much alcohol. We also try to avoid or numb the pain in our lives, despite warnings of the consequences from loved ones or physicians. We are a society that prefers to call problematic behaviour someone else's fault. We choose not to be responsible for our choices and prefer that someone or something outside of us fix us. Yes, we make choices that will kill us sooner than necessary. As long as we kill ourselves slowly, some of us can still judge the suicide victims, and tell ourselves that it's okay for us to do so.

Some people believe that mental illness can be prayed away, similar to the bigoted belief that we can somehow "pray away the gay"; that with the right prayers, God will take away any "affliction." If I suffered with severe depression and felt that there was no way out except death, I would have faith that my family would do something tangible rather than suggest Bible readings. I have loved ones that I know would pray, and I would be grateful for the kind gesture, but I would be most grateful if they compassionately intervened with the assistance of mental health professionals. A quote from the famous American entertainer Gypsy Rose Lee comes to mind; "Praying is like a rocking chair - it'll give you something to do, but it won't get you anywhere."

I remember hearing a few years ago that a man I knew growing up took his own life. Perhaps it is a sign of progress in a Catholic world where suicide is an unforgivable sin that the Catholic priest chose to perform the prayer service—an act probably more consistent with what Jesus would do. This man was suffering to such an extent that he could not bear to suffer any longer. I can imagine no sadder state of a fellow human being and of grieving Catholic families that are left believing that there is no destination other than hell for the soul of their loved one.

Divorce for Catholics

It's a no-no. Marriage is forever, regardless of the reasons for the breakdown in the marriage, even if there was any type of abuse: you made your bed, you sleep in it, is the deal according to Catholicism. The Bible is very clear on this one: When you marry someone, according to Mark 10:8, *you are no longer two, but one flesh.* Mark 10:9 reads, *What therefore God has joined together, let no man separate.* A few verses later in Mark 10:11-12, he increases the stakes with: *Whoever divorces his wife and marries another woman commits adultery against her; and if she herself divorces her husband and marries another man, she is committing adultery.*

Despite the threats in the book of Mark, things had not worked out for my first marriage and we went through the painful process of divorce. It was a difficult time for everyone involved and despite some inevitable regrets, two amazing kids were the result of the union.

Incidentally, I was told shortly after I became a divorcee, "Thanks, but someone else will take over leading the youth group at the church." It didn't hit me until then that I was no longer really welcome in the Catholic Church, that it took the divorce rules of the Bible seriously. I took it personally and stopped going to that church, where I had been involved with my family for several years.

My former husband and I both moved on in our lives. My current marriage of almost sixteen years is to Murray, a man who has never been involved in religion. At the time I met him, I knew that he had been baptized, even if *only* as an Anglican, so as far as his soul was concerned, there might be some wiggle room on judgment day. He knew that being involved in a church community was important to me so he participated wholeheartedly in our mission to find another church after I felt no longer welcome in my original one. Not only was I divorced, but even worse according to the Catholic rules, I had re-married outside of the Catholic Church so I was officially a wayward or a *fallen away* Catholic. These were the compassionate labels in the church at that time. If I wanted back into the church, I would be required to go through the annulment process, which was costly and made little sense to me. The priest claimed that it was a way of working through the things that went wrong in the marriage, which made some sense if a person hadn't done so before moving on, but this growth process would also cost between one and two thousand dollars. However, I respected this soft-spoken kind priest and really wanted his approval and to be welcomed back into the church community. A provincial tribunal would study my case, my story and the possibility that I had not entered into the marriage freely.

I survived this strange process and, with the payment of twelve hundred dollars, was granted an annulment. My marriage was declared officially null and void, and had never happened in the Church's eyes. So strong was my indoctrination that I couldn't stop there. I convinced Murray that our marriage should be blessed in the Catholic Church. It happened soon after, in a small, private ceremony. To completely clean the slate, I decided that our son from this marriage would be baptized in the Church as well. He had been dedicated in the Alliance Church but the nagging feeling remained with me that a dedication is not enough to ensure safe passage to heaven. I felt obligated to complete this last required task for my son's soul. I still wanted to belong, but even more, I wanted desperately to avoid hell. I had all the guilt associated with being Catholic but little if any of the comfort that I once enjoyed.

Chapter 4

Convinced by the Pope

> *She [the Catholic Church] worked hard at it night and day during nine centuries and imprisoned, tortured, hanged, and burned whole hordes and armies of witches, and washed the Christian world clean with their foul blood. Then they discovered that there was no such thing as witches, and never had been. One doesn't know whether to laugh or cry. Who discovered that there was no such thing as a witch—the priest the parson? No, these never discover anything...*—Mark Twain

For years I felt intense guilt for failing in the obligation as a Catholic parent to instil a strong faith in my children. It seemed a chore to get everyone up and ready to go to church, but doing so was the only thing that would relieve the guilt. Even after fulfilling the obligatory hour of church once a week, I felt guilty for not praying at home with my family and for not bringing them up in a more devout way. I felt responsible for their souls and I was not properly preparing them to avoid hell. Maybe praying as a family felt strange and uncomfortable because I grew up without talking about God and religion as a family.

My feelings of failure and guilt slowly turned to relief when I realized the positive result of not indoctrinating my children. They grew up knowing very little about the Bible and thankfully never accepted the doctrine of original sin (that we are born sinful and must earn our way to heaven). They are generous, kind, moral human beings and are able to see and question the injustices and inconsistencies of religion without any deep-seated guilt weighing down their ability to critically do so. The motivation of their goodness is not to earn a spot in a heavenly afterlife. They are good people for their own sakes. I am not sorry that I failed to convince them to adhere to the archaic rules of a Church established by homophobic, misogynistic men in the Bronze Age.

Had I done a better job as a Catholic mother, they might have grown up with less of an ability, and probably desire, to think critically about the impact of religion in their lives. Even though the church represented all things comforting and loving for the first four decades of my life, I was starting to see how all of that time, I had been naive or foolish for believing that Catholics were special. The sense of specialness faded rather quickly as I learned more about the Church, and knew that I could not be a part of what it stood for in its sordid history or even in my lifetime.

One of the most impressive accounts I found addressing my growing concerns was an Intelligence Squared Debate that included Stephen Fry and Christopher Hitchens in 2009.[3] I became embarrassed, then angry. The more that I

---

[3]   Intelligence Squared Debate 2009, accessed on April 14, 2012, www.intelligencesquared.com/events/catholic-church -United Kingdom

dug through the dogma, the more I saw beliefs that I had always taken for granted turned upside down. The more I looked into what was going on in the Catholic Church, the more upset I became with the likely possibility that there was truth to the claims of sexism, intolerance and child rape. I was starting to see a horrific mess perpetrated at the hands of none other than the leader. It was time to look to the pope for some answers. What does the leader of the One True Church really stand for in the 21st century?

Our Vicar of Christ on Earth

The pope, who lives in marble and gold, was supposed to be the only infallible human being on earth—but as I researched further, this became disappointingly not so. Sometimes, I got so angry I couldn't write about what I was learning; it was too overwhelming to a woman, to a mother.

Based on the pope's direction and guidance, women were supposed to remain in their rightful place—as servants in the church. The patriarchal hierarchy of the Church includes no women and no men with wives or daughters. That is archaic to say the least. I sat through two beautiful weddings during one of the summers that I was writing. During each ceremony I heard the words of Ephesians 5: *Wives submit to your husbands as to the Lord. For the husband is the head of the wife as Christ is the head of the church, his body, of which he is the Saviour. Now as the church submits to Christ, so also wives should submit to their husbands in everything.*

I thought about other tenets of the belief system. The intolerant attitude toward homosexuality came to mind. The biblical view of homosexuals, although never mentioned by Jesus, and only in the Old Testament, is still shared in the world today. *Thou shalt not lie with mankind, as with womankind: it is abomination . . .* Leviticus 18:22. The National Catholic Register reported on a September 5, 2002 speech given by Pope John Paul II, that stated sexually disordered men are not appropriate candidates for the priesthood:

> ". . . It would be lamentable if, out of a misunderstood tolerance, they ordained young men who are immature or have obvious signs of affective deviations that, as is sadly known, could cause serious anomalies in the consciences of the faithful, with evident damage for the whole Church. "[4]

"Affective deviations" is really referring to "disordered" sexual orientations. According to Cardinal Jorge Arturo Medina Estevez, retired prefect for the Congregation for Divine Worship and the Discipline of the Sacraments, the ordination of homosexual men is: ". . . absolutely inadvisable and imprudent, and from the pastoral point of view, very risky. A homosexual person or someone with homosexual tendencies is not, therefore, suitable to receive the sacrament of holy orders."[5]

---

[4]   Wayne Laugesen. "U.S. Bishops to Begin Inspecting Catholic Seminaries", accessed April 28, 2012. http://www.beliefnet. com/News/2002/12/U-S-Bishops-To-Begin-Inspecting-Catholic-Seminaries.aspx

[5]   Austin Cline, "Priests in the Roman Catholic Church," accessed April 14, 2012 http://atheism.about.com/od/catholic ismandgays/a/gaypriests.htm.

Something that I never could quite understand was how a perfect Creator could create fellow human beings as *morally evil*—as our current leader of the Catholic Church regards homosexual people. Why would God miss-wire a considerable segment of our population just to endure the judgments that his *good* book outlines for them? This is not tolerance. We hear too many stories about gay bullying and resultant teenage suicides. Eventually Catholics will have to regard homosexual people as people deserving of respect.

The saying "Love the sinner, hate the sin" is somehow meant to make homosexuals feel accepted and deserving. As growing up Catholic resulted in my own internal struggles with sin and guilt, I cannot imagine the possibly larger effect that the Church has had and continues to have on people who are not heterosexual. It is not my business how a loving consenting couple express their love. I am probably not the only one who finds this somewhat ironic coming from a church hierarchy who chose to turn a blind eye for decades to systematic child rape within its organization.

I came across the horrifying evidence in an article "Catholic Church Sex Abuse Scandals Around the World" highlighting the cases of child sex abuse, and what was being done to compensate the victims and to bring the perpetrators to justice. Johann Hari, a columnist with one of Britain's leading newspapers, the *Independent*, wrote not only about the priests who raped children, but about the cover-up and lack of response from the church hierarchy, blaming the current pope:

> For over 25 years, Ratzinger was personally in charge of the Congregation for the Doctrine of the Faith, the part of the Vatican responsible for enforcing Catholic canonical law across the world,

including sexual abuse . . . We know what the methods of the church were during this period. When it was discovered a child had been raped by a priest, the church swore everybody involved to secrecy, and moved the priest on to another parish. When he raped more children, they too were sworn to secrecy, and he was moved on to another parish . . . and on, and on. Over 10,000 people have come forward to say they were raped as part of this misery-go-round. The church insisted all cases be kept from the police and dealt with by their own 'canon' law—which can only 'punish' child-rapists to prayer or penitence or, on rare occasions, defrocking. In 2001, Ratzinger wrote to every bishop in the world, telling them allegations of abuse must be dealt with 'in absolute secrecy . . . completely suppressed by perpetual silence. [6]

During my research, I also discovered organizations established specifically to assist the victims of child rape in churches: Survivors Network of Those Abused by Priests (www.snapnetwork.org) and Bishop Accountability (www. bishopaccountability.org). I was disgusted, not with the websites, but because there was a worldwide need for sites like these. The degree that the abuse was hidden, ignored, and perpetuated, as these holy men were moved from parish to parish of unsuspecting parents and children is unbelievable. And it continues today. The website has an Abuse Tracker

---

[6] Johann Hari, "Catholics—shun the Pope who has abused you," accessed April 14, 2012. http://www.johannhari. com/2010/09/09/

which shows recent charges and new convictions worldwide. These are not support networks for survivors of tsunamis or other natural disasters but for victims of the supposedly most *moral*, holy men in positions of trust.

During this time of learning about the decades-long, rape of children in the Catholic Church and subsequent cover up around the world, I was provided with a more local perspective. A junior hockey coach was convicted of sexually assaulting teenaged male hockey players in 1997, and there had been an outcry in our province. With shock and disbelief, we read the details of repeated sexual assaults over the course of several years. This monster had set himself up to have easy access to young boys and took advantage of his powerful position as their coach. Unsuspecting families had sent their talented boys to be preyed upon. Considering the lives that he affected and the horrific impact of his offences, his sentence was short—only three and a half years in jail. I was told, "See, sexual scandals involving children happen in every occupation."

This was awful of course, but priests not only had the common focus of working with minors from a position of trust, but were to be respected and revered not just as teachers but as holy men personally appointed by God. The hockey coach, after having been found out, was not just moved along to another junior hockey team with new teenage boys to abuse. Imagine the outrage if excuses had been made for the coach or if the players had been sworn to secrecy with hush money from local hockey communities. Clearly, no other organization's response to child rape was more irresponsible or immoral than the response of the Catholic Church.

As a Catholic woman, I was embarrassed seeing the weakened credibility of the Church. I heard Catholics suggest that some kids were lying about the abuse but a quick look at the Survivors Network of those Abused by Priests and the thousands of abuse cases around the world indicates a widespread systemic problem in the One True Church. How the Church continues to respond to this institutional practice is indefensible. I had to wonder why, as Catholics, we seemed more concerned about these "attacks" on the Church, than about the children who were abused.

In September 2011, the current pope, along with two other high ranking Holy See officials, were finally, formally, accused of crimes against humanity by the victims of sex abuse. The complaint was made to the international criminal court, with the submission including: failing to prevent or punish perpetrators of rape and sexual violence and engaging in the widespread practice of concealing sexual crimes around the world. [7]

More hypocrisy from the Catholic front:

I was shocked to learn that the Catholic Church did not allow African women with promiscuous husbands to protect themselves by the use of condoms. In this significant way, the pope and his church were clearly failing humanity—in my opinion. Joseph Daleiden, the famous author who wrote *The Science of Morality: The Individual Community and Future Generations*, explains the extensive damage that has been the result of the pope's opposition to contraception

---

[7] Michael Stone, "Pope Benedict XVI charged with crimes against humanity." accessed April 14, 2012. http://www. examiner.com/humanist-in-national/pope-benedict-xvi-charged-with-crimes-against-humanity, *Examiner.com*.

use including 55 million abortions performed in the world annually, with 182,000 women dying each year from dangerous abortions.[8]

Contradictions and controversies continued to surface and/or I began to pay more attention to them. A few decades ago the Church finally sainted Mary Magdalene and allowed its depiction of her as a prostitute to fade. Thanks to provocative novelists such as Dan Brown, the Divine Feminine had resurfaced among mainstream society. I was slowly realizing just how much things veered off track about 2000 years ago with the men in power at the time deciding which books to include in the Bible. Was Mary Magdalene never really a prostitute as she was referred to when I was a child? I learned the story about how forgiveness is available to everyone, even someone as sinful as a prostitute. Jesus loved her in the story, we were told, not in a romantic way but in a manner of pure unconditional love. This story had given me great comfort over the years—because it would at times soften the deeply engrained guilt associated with something as normal and natural as sex. I will share more of my journey surrounding this mysterious female friend of Jesus later.

I was shocked to learn of another side to Mother Teresa, an icon in the Catholic Church, someone on the fast track to sainthood. Apparently, she might not have been the selfless woman that I was led to believe as a Catholic. According to Christopher Hitchens, who captures her true essence in his book called *The Missionary Position*, she was addicted to suffering, not for herself, but for others. She is said to have withheld medical attention for people under her care, people

---

8   Joseph Daleiden. Quote found on http://calgaryhumanist. ca/ericsquotes.html, accessed April 28, 2012.

who were dying painful deaths. Her millions were spent on nunneries and monasteries rather than hospitals and pain medication. She had six million dollars in a Vatican account when she died. On her deathbed, as she laid suffering in a modern hospital, she denounced her faith. I found I could no longer refer to someone who is selfless and generous as "Mother Teresa," as it would be more accurately an insult.

After all this, all I could imagine is that if Jesus were to return to observe the Vatican, if he saw the selfishness and greed of the Church, if he saw the treatment of women, homosexuals, the cover-up of child rape, the hypocrisy of his representation on earth, the children who were sworn to secrecy after being raped, and the priests who were moved from parish to parish, he might be the first to leave the Church.

I didn't think I could remain part of the Church once I learned of its brutal history and the continuing injustices and atrocities, even though I saw how many people could apparently live a peaceful religious life without questioning their faith. I do acknowledge the wonderful moderate and relatively progressive Catholic people I know, whose generosity and kindness would undoubtedly exist with or without religion. I admired Catholic parents who, for instance, unconditionally love their gay children, despite the intolerance of their religious leadership.

It is my sincere hope that the faithful who sit in the pews next to friends who have gay children suspend their bigotry and judgment and recognize that these views say much more about the devout, than it says about gay Catholics. I hope that they challenge their Vicar of Christ and his message that our gay friends and neighbours are disordered, morally evil individuals. I offer this as another example of how religion has done the devil's finest work.

Nowhere has there been more divisiveness, wars, bigotry, sexism, and judgment than in the name of religion, and unfortunately it continues today.

* * *

> *Religion is fundamentally opposed to everything I hold in veneration—courage, clear thinking, honesty, fairness, and, above all, love of the truth.*—H.L. Mencken

As I sat in a pew of my childhood church, waiting for a funeral service to begin, I picked up a blue pamphlet from the little hymnal holder in front of me. It was titled, *Communion Guidelines*. A gasp escaped my mouth when I read: "We also welcome to this celebration those Christians from other denominations who are not fully united with us. It is a consequence of the sad divisions in Christianity that we cannot extend to you a general invitation to receive Holy Communion for this would imply a oneness which does not exist, and for which we must all pray."

How horrible! First, I suspected that not everyone who visited that church was Christian. Hindus, Muslims, Sikhs, Jehovah Witnesses, Jews, and even agnostics or atheists might attend from time to time, especially for funerals or weddings. Second, it was implying that responsibility for the divisiveness in Christianity lies with the *other* Christians, when the Catholics are the ones who claim that theirs is the One True Church in the world.

At this point in my research and life, when I heard someone say that they were Catholic, I wanted to respond, "Oh dear, I'm so sorry." I was no longer feeling the love. I thought that perhaps I could just switch to Lutheranism.

A part of me still yearned for a church and religion with a foundation and a long history. If it could no longer be Catholicism, I needed to find a different Christian church. I was attracted to how Martin Luther had had the courage to split from the Catholic Church, and for logical reasons concerning indulgences, intermediaries, and celibacy. But then I read further about Martin Luther and his anti-Semitism: "His vehement attack on Jews and his powerful influence on the German faithful has brought a new hypothesis to mind: that the Jewish holocaust, and indeed, the eliminationist form of anti-Semitism in Nazi Germany may not have occurred without the influence from Luther's book *On the Jews and Their Lies. In Mein Kampf*, Hitler listed Martin Luther as one of the greatest reformers."[9] Luther's quotes indicate how he really felt about women as well: "No marital duty takes place without sin. Wives are to be beaten. If they [women] become tired or even die in child-birth that is why they are there."[10]

What about just being a Christian in the general sense, I wondered? Unfortunately the original problem remained, with the Bible and with Christianity in general. My brave venture outside of the Church had been delayed many times due to the little voice in my Catholic head telling me that this very act of searching other belief systems meant doubt,

---

[9] Jim Walker, "Martin Luther's dirty little book: On the Jews and their lies. A precursor to Nazism" (1996, 2005), accessed May 27, 2012, on the website http://www.nobeliefs.com/luther.htm

[10] Dean R Dowling, "Witch-Hunts and The Christian Mentality" (2000), accessed May 27, 2012 on websites: http://ed5015.tripod.com/ReligWitchhunts71.htm, and http://www.thewisemag.com/mystery/item/96-devils-wine

lack of faith, and worst of all, sin. It was a sure sign of lack of faith to question faith, or to question why we believe.

*   *   *

"So, are you still anti-Catholic?" a friend asked recently at the hair salon. I was a bit startled by the question. "Oh God no!" I said, "I am pro equal treatment for all people, male and female (heterosexual or not), against indoctrinating children with deprecatory messages of original sin and abusive threats of hell, against fallible male church leaders dictating what we do with our bodies, against one of the richest organizations in the world enjoying tax breaks, and against government funding of Catholic schools that discourage condom use or other forms of birth control." I also explained that I am against the Church's judgment of non-Catholics, the belief that their church is the One True Church, and that devout believers of different faiths all over the world are destined for hell.

Chapter 5

To Swear on the Bible

Properly read, the Bible is the most potent force for atheism ever conceived.—Isaac Asimov

I was at work one day when visited by a police officer who asked my name and then handed me a piece of paper. It was a subpoena to appear in court as an expert witness. This wasn't the first time that I'd been required to do this, but this time my mind went immediately to the part where you must swear an oath on the Bible. The subpoena read:

> **NOTICE**: When you come to court you will be offered the choice of swearing an oath or making an affirmation before you give your evidence. An affirmation is a nonreligious promise to tell the truth. If you wish to give evidence other than by making an affirmation or swearing an oath on the Christian Bible, please feel free to bring with you any religious symbol or Holy Book and advise the clerk prior to court commencing about the oath you wish to take.

In the past I'd not thought twice about doing this but now I had a better idea of what was in the religious book. I had some new and serious questions about this practice that supposedly holds a person to the truth "so help me God," as it used to be said, although now only expressed in old movies and television shows. Would my integrity and honesty be questioned if I chose the alternative available? Was this alternative subtly viewed as suspect by the courts? Why would swearing on the Bible guarantee truth-telling when most people probably don't know what's in the book?

I felt compelled to do further research behind a practice that combined a 2,000-year-old religious book and the legal system. According to Wikipedia, "The first personage in the biblical tradition to take an oath is held to be Eliezer, the chief servant of Abraham, when the latter requested of the former that he not take a wife for his son Isaac from the daughters of Canaan, but rather from among Abraham's own family. In the Judeo-Christian Tradition, this is held as the origination of the concept that it is required to hold a sacred object in one's hand when taking an oath." [11] I suspect that taking an oath may have been even more potent when people were afraid to be struck down by God if they did not tell the truth.

On the day that I was to testify, I was still weighing the options of either going along with the status quo and swearing on the book or stepping out and committing my first act of what a small part of me still viewed as blasphemy. I was more nervous about the oath than fulfilling my duties as a witness! I practiced the affirmation in my mind so that I wouldn't mess up my first small but public act of rebellion.

[11]   http://en.wikipedia.org/wiki/Oath, accessed April 14, 2012.

I felt that I could no longer swear on a book that had no more credibility for me than a novel.

When I asked several theists how they know what they know about religious matters, the response sometimes was that "the Bible says so." I had to wonder, had God *really* inspired men to write this moral guide, so that we would know what he wants us to do, how to serve, obey, and praise him? Moderate Catholics don't believe in the literal sense of the Bible, fortunately. We generally took from it the good stuff and ignored the not-so-good. When I started to read it carefully on my own, I found I had not clearly remembered the details of the Old Testament or the senseless brutality of the God described within. Here are just a few examples of the parts that I had forgotten or disregarded:

> *Happy those who seize your children and smash them against a rock.* Psalm 137:9.

> *Slaves, be subject to your masters with all reverence, not only to those who are good, and equitable but also to those who are perverse.* 1 Peter 2:18.

> *Behold now, I have two daughters which have not known man; let me, I pray you, bring them out unto you, and do ye unto them as is good in your eyes, only unto these men do nothing.* Genesis 19:8.

> *Their children also be dashed to pieces before their eyes; their houses shall be spoiled, and their wives ravished.* Isaiah 13:16.

The God in the Bible advocates slavery, genocide, killing children, and selling daughters as slaves or for sexual pleasure. He chose sides in war—even though each side believed without a doubt that he was on their side. He advocated the killing of homosexuals, of witches, and of women who are unfaithful.

Thou shalt not suffer a witch to live. Exodus 22:18

I was especially shocked to read that killing witches had been encouraged in the Old Testament. Then, I discovered the horrific consequences of this biblical message in our not-so-distant history. I read about the treatise, Malleus Maleficarum (Latin for Hammer of Witches). It was written in 1486 by Heinrich Kramer and Jacob Sprenger, published in Germany in 1487, and commended by Pope Innocent. Its main purpose was to challenge all arguments against the existence of witchcraft and to instruct magistrates on how to identify, interrogate and convict witches. It was a how-to-guide to prosecuting and killing them.

Why would God give us divine permission to do such horrible things? In a book, *The Demon Haunted World*, author and scientist Carl Sagan writes this about *The Malleus Maleficarum:* "With exhaustive citations of Scripture and of ancient and modern scholars, they produced The *Malleus Maleficarum*, the 'Hammer of Witches'—aptly described as one of the most terrifying documents in human history."[12]

Sagan describes how the accused or her relatives had to pay for the costs of the investigation, the trial and the execution, including "per diems for the private detectives hired to spy on her, wine for her guards, banquets for her

[12] Transcribed by Wicasta Lovelace and Christie Jury, "Carl Sagan And The Malleus Maleficarum," posted August 24, 2009, accessed April 21, 2012 http://www.malleusmaleficarum.org/

judges, the travel expenses of a messenger sent to fetch a more experienced torturer from another city, and the faggots, tar and hangman's rope."[13] If she had any property, it was divided between Church and State.

> The more who, under torture, confessed to witchcraft, the harder it was to maintain that the whole business was mere fantasy. Since each "witch" was made to implicate others, the numbers grew exponentially. These constituted "frightful proofs that the Devil is still alive," as it was later put in America in the Salem witch trials. In a credulous age, the most fantastic testimony was soberly accepted—that tens of thousands of witches had gathered for a Sabbath in public squares in France, or that 12,000 of them darkened the skies as they flew to Newfoundland . . . Legions of women were burnt to death. And the most horrendous tortures were routinely applied to every defendant, young or old, after the instruments of torture were first blessed by the priests. [Pope] Innocent himself died in 1492, following unsuccessful attempts to keep him alive by transfusion (which resulted in the deaths of three boys) and by suckling at the breast of a nursing mother, He was mourned by his mistress and their children.[14]

*   *   *

---

[13]   See note 12.
[14]   See note 12.

I decided to ask some theists if they really knew what the Old Testament said and their response was that it doesn't mean anything anymore; it's just the New Testament that's relevant now. Then one of them added, "Oh yes, other than the Ten Commandments that are believed to be the *actual* word of God." I noted that one third of the commandments referred to God being honoured and worshipped and have nothing to do with morality or ethics. The God of the Old Testament threatened a torturous hell if he wasn't honoured and obeyed. Determining the *moral* law of the land, he sounded more like a dictator than a loving Father.

I was shocked to read other contradictions too, including the two different renditions of the Ten Commandments: the list in Exodus 20 and the one in Exodus 34. Which set were we commanded to follow? Rarely did I, or anyone near me, keep the Sabbath holy, despite the clear unwavering guidelines of these commandments. The Sabbath is interpreted differently, and begins on different days depending on the holy book so I wondered which was right. The commandments sounded sillier as I broke them down. Would I consider murder without knowing the commandment? Many non-religious people seemed to live moral lives without these ancient guidelines.

It would not be productive for me to criticize the commandments without providing some alternative that would be more relevant to the 21st century. I would suggest commandments that would forbid murder, slavery, child rape or other types of abuse toward children, abuse or sexual assault of any kind, sexism or homophobia, and racism.

*   *   *

When I asked theists how they could be so sure about their religious beliefs, they qualified with the usual "Well, the Bible says . . ." I then had to ask which bible, and which translation? There are thousands of versions. The water could not get any muddier! Using the Bible—a book written by men several decades or more after Jesus died—for argument's sake had become invalid for me. I was discovering numerous inconsistencies and contradictions. To my embarrassment, I had honestly thought that Matthew, Mark, Luke and John were Jesus' best friends, his *Facebook* friends of the time! I was shocked to learn that they did not even live at the same time. The jury is out on who the authors of the Bible really were; no one knows if the books are historical truth or merely fictional stories. I was surprised to learn that the gospel *truth* has not been proven by any actual evidence. Maybe I was just not reading it correctly; after all I am not a learned scholar or theologian, but even they can't agree on what is really meant by the scriptures!

The Bible may have been the best resource for that time, but how truly great would a book be that was actually written by a real god of love? It is instead possibly the worst book on morality that I have ever read, certainly not appropriate for bedtime reading to my children. I understand that the stories might have been consistent with the morality of the time of writing. This was an age when women were without rights and perhaps this is where the pope's view of women comes from. According to Elizabeth Cady Stanton, "The Bible and the Church have been the greatest stumbling blocks in the way of woman's emancipation." When I tried to find where our current pope's views may have originated in the Bible, I found the following:

But I would have you know, that the head of every man is Christ; and the head of the woman is the man; and the head of Christ is God. I Corinthians 11:3

For the man is not of the woman; but the woman of the man. Neither was the man created for the woman; but the woman for the man. I Corinthians 11:8-9

Let the women learn in silence with all subjection. But I suffer not a woman to teach, nor to usurp authority over the man, but to be in silence. For Adam was first formed, then Eve. And Adam was not deceived, but the woman being deceived was in the transgression. I Timothy 2:11-14

Wives, submit yourselves unto your own husbands, as unto the Lord. For the husband is the head of the wife, even as Christ is the head of the Church: and he is the saviour of the body. Therefore as the church is subject unto Christ, so let the wives be to their own husbands in everything. Ephesians 5:22-24

Let your women keep silence in the churches: for it is not permitted unto them to speak; but they are commanded to be under obedience, as also saith the law. And if they will learn anything, let them ask their husbands at home: for it is a shame for women to speak in the church. I Corinthians 14:34-35. [Paul in the New Testament was really not a friend of the opposite sex.]

> *Unto the woman he said, I will greatly multiply thy sorrow and thy conception; in sorrow thou shalt bring forth children; and thy desire shall be to thy husband, and he shall rule over thee.* Genesis 3:16

As I read the moral code of Christianity, the divine havoc continued with its endorsement of stoning women, killing children, slavery, and torture. I had expected it to promote more of the values that I practice every day; tolerance, equality, knowledge, reason, humanity, and kindness.

Elizabeth Cady Stanton sums up the Bible's position with regards to women: "The Bible teaches that women brought sin and death into the world, that she precipitated the fall of the race, that she was arraigned before the judgment seat of Heaven, tried, condemned and sentenced. Marriage for her was to be a condition of bondage, maternity a period of suffering and anguish, and in silence and subjection, she was to play the role of a dependent on man's bounty for all her material wants . . ."[15]

* * *

I kept hearing these wise words in my head, "If you don't believe in something, you will fall for anything." Ironically, it was a fellow theist who cautioned me with this statement, and it was while I was a person of faith that I had believed many extraordinary things without question. As it turned out, this was the time when I had been most gullible. As cautious as I was about extraordinary claims, I was

---

[15]   Elizabeth Cady Stanton quoted in the website The Dark Bible, Women's Inferior Status, accessed April 28, 2012. http://www.nobeliefs.com/DarkBible/darkbible7.htm

discovering that it was finally okay to think critically about religion and the Bible. I had to seriously question how a God could inspire such brutality and terror, as in the Old Testament. I remembered the New Testament differently and waded through it again, anticipating the love, compassion, equality, respect, and peace preached in my childhood. I had read the stories so many times in the past that I was desensitized and never thought to question the validity of a virgin giving birth, a man resurrecting from the dead, a blind man seeing again, people turning into pillars of salt, or someone turning water to wine. Besides, we were not to question what we were taught.

At this juncture in my journey, I found an article by Joseph McCabe called "The Myth of the Resurrection," from 1925 that outlined the many inconsistencies and contradictions within the Holy Scriptures. It was one of the most convincing articles pertaining to the fallacy of the Bible that I found over the course of my research.

WWJD?

Whenever I would hear a Christian say or do something not particularly *Christ-like*, I liked to respond with the common mantra, What Would Jesus Do (WWJD)? I suppose it might have been a passive-aggressive way of suggesting that, for someone supposedly religious, the person was acting surprisingly rude, selfish, or mean.

This led me to think about what would happen if Jesus stopped by for a visit today. He would undoubtedly be shocked and heartbroken to reflect on the Inquisition, the Crusades, the Holocaust, and stories of slavery and oppression. Jesus visiting us now might even cry, "WHAT

THE HELL! What have you been doing for the past 2000 years?" He would probably want to know how we could have ever thought that this is what he meant when he said that all are made equal, and to respect and love one another. I think he would be appalled at the treatment of women, children, and of people who are different in some way. Undoubtedly, he would scold us for the mess we have made, and be disappointed to see the treatment of women as servants of man, and the Bible-based bullying of gay people. I imagined he would be disappointed about so much killing on earth in the name of religion.

If he returned, Jesus would be surprised about the once common practice of burning people merely for possessing, reading, and translating the Bible into English. Thomas More was a prominent Catholic who was involved in actions against such heretics at the time of the Reformation: "As Lord Chancellor, he had imprisoned and interrogated Lutherans, sometimes in his own house, and sent six reformers to be burned at the stake . . ."[16] He was sainted recently by the Catholic Church.

I suspect that an ideal Jesus would prefer that the Church be a place of support and love, not rampant abuse and pedophilia by its leaders. But then I started to read passages in the New Testament about the not-so-kind side of Jesus. There were days when he was less a Prince of Peace, and more a tyrant. In Luke 21:16 *Jesus himself will cause your family and your household to be torn apart.* These are just a few more examples:

---

[16] James Wood, "The Broken Estate: Essays on Literature and Belief," accessed April 14, 2012. New York: Random House, 1999. 3-15. http://www.luminarium.org/renlit/wood.htm

> *Brother shall deliver up the brother to death, and*
> *the father the child: and the children shall rise up*
> *against their parents, and cause them to be put to*
> *death.* Matthew 10:21

When Jesus is criticized by the Pharisees for not washing his hands before eating, he defends himself by attacking them for not killing disobedient children according to the commandment: *He that curseth father or mother, let him die the death.* Matthew 15:4-7

In Matthew 19:29, Jesus asks that his followers abandon their children to follow him and in Mark 7:9, he criticizes the Jews for not killing their disobedient children according to Old Testament law. In Mark 4:25, Jesus says that those who have been less fortunate in this life will have it even worse in the life to come. Mark 4:25

Jesus condemns entire cities to dreadful deaths and to the eternal torment of hell because they didn't care for his preaching in Matthew 11:20, and in Luke 12:47, he allows the beating of slaves.

In Mark 5:12:13, Jesus sends the devils into 2000 pigs, causing them to jump off a cliff and be drowned in the sea. Clearly Jesus could have simply sent the devils out, yet he chose instead to place them into pigs and kill them. Mark 5:12-13

* * *

I used to admire the most devout people, the ones who had a strong faith and adhered to all of the teachings of the Bible. Then I realized that the theists I know are really just day-to-day peace-loving Christians, who were not truly adhering to the Bible. If they were, they would be busy doing all of the horrific things that God demands of them. I decided I should not be critical of the moderates or those referred to as 'cafeteria Catholics,' picking and choosing from the Bible menu. It is the most religiously devout, we should be worried about, as Sam Harris points out: 'The men who committed the atrocities of September 11 were certainly not 'cowards,' as they were repeatedly described in the Western media, nor were they lunatics in any ordinary sense. They were men of faith—perfect faith, as it turns out—and this, it must finally be acknowledged, is a terrible thing to be."[17]

In the end I knew that I personally choose not to kill, lie, steal, or covet, not because the Ten Commandments *command* so, but because I would prefer to live in peace, without conflict and as much as possible, to help and not hurt others. I try to follow the Golden Rule—do unto others as you would have others do unto you—which I learned was introduced to society long before the major religions. As early as the seventh century BCE, the Greek philosopher Pittacus invoked the Golden Rule.[18] I had always thought that morality came from religion. Fortunately the Golden Rule could encompass all of the commandments important to me as well as serve as a general guideline for morality.

---

[17]   Sam Harris, *The End of Faith: Religion, Terror, and the Future of Reason.* (New York, W. W. Norton & Company, Inc., 2004), 67.

[18]   http://www.cleverbadger.net/wordpress/page/46/?m=wqntz nggytrqnil&googleb0t=true

Morality—I sleep with it every night.

> **With or without religion, you would have good people doing good things and evil people doing evil things. But for good people to do evil things, that takes religion.**—Steven Weinberg, Nobel Laureate in Physics

As I struggled with my long-held belief system, I began to question what I had once taken for granted—the idea that we couldn't be moral without religion. A discussion with Murray (who had never read any bible) finally brought clarity to my confusion. I turned to him one day while we were watching one of our sons play volleyball and asked, "So, what do you feel guilty about?"

"Nothing."

"Really?" I asked but he repeated his answer. "How can you not feel guilty about anything?" I asked.

"What about regrets?" I asked.

"Of course there are some things that I wish that I had done differently, but nothing that I feel guilty about."

"So no guilt . . . what's that like?" He really didn't understand the burden of deeply engrained guilt. How could someone not understand guilt? I tried another question. "So, why do you do the good things that you do for people?" (Ty, our youngest son, had written an essay in school on why his dad is his hero, listing the many things that he witnessed him doing, often for perfect strangers. On several occasions he has come across accidents, life-threatening situations or simply people stranded on the highway, and always made the necessary effort to assist.)

He answered, "Because that's just what people do—it's the right thing to do."

"Well, how do YOU know the right thing to do?" I challenged.

"We are all human beings and I try not to hurt anyone and to help people when I can."

I thought to myself that it could not really be that simple—how did he actually know this without any knowledge of the Bible or the Ten Commandments? I clarified, "So you don't do these things to get to heaven or to avoid hell?"

He laughed because he hadn't grown up believing in a religion or a god so he didn't understand the concept of an afterlife. He thought it was kind of ridiculous and I must admit so did I, once I heard myself say it out loud. After all, if getting a payoff in the afterlife is your main motivation for doing good, that is indeed less than virtuous.

I had truly believed that morality came only from religion: the arrogant and erroneous claim of religion that we would not know right from wrong, we would rape and murder without the threat of hell or obeisance of the laws in the Bible. Shouldn't morality be about alleviating unnecessary suffering, rather than about heaven and hell or saints and sinners?

While reconsidering my beliefs, I thought about the people who I had once perceived as moral: the pope, church leaders, and the kind people of faith. Without speaking up, they all seemed to be supporting the misogyny, the pedophilia and the cover-up, the irresponsible deadly messages about condom use, the judgments about homosexual people, and about terrifying children with hellfire.

It would be immoral for me to remain silent about such religious beliefs and practices that cause harm. With or without religion, I cherish my life and want to live peacefully with others. I was realizing that most of religion no longer made sense to me; it was irrational to believe, that because it says so in the Bible, it must be true. God could have done a much better job if he truly was omnipotent (all-powerful), omniscient (all-knowing); if he had written the Book or inspired it. It became more and more difficult for me to believe any of it, even if we could pick and choose the good stuff and leave the not-so-good. Who chooses what is really true? How faithful was I if I would only adhere to the more positive parts of the Bible? Most people will tell you that the New Testament with Jesus is the new and improved testament. But I had to wonder then, why still use the Bible to bully homosexual people when homosexuality is only mentioned in the "not-as-relevant" Old Testament? We gave up burning witches when the enlightened of the time realized that witches did not exist; we abolished slavery, but not without a fight from Bible literalists, and religious or not, we end our marriages without really believing what the Bible says about the dire consequences of doing so.

If the Bible is regarded as it really ought to be—a two-thousand-year-old book written by men with barbaric customs in ancient times—then there can be no rewards or punishments, other than the personal consequences of the choices we make every day. I now strongly believe that how we live our lives, how we treat each other, how we take care of ourselves, and how we take responsibility for our choices is really what matters.

Location! Location! Location!

I had said from a very young age that I didn't want to go to hell on a technicality—but I was now finding an abundance of technicalities. The only reason that I became a Christian or a Catholic was because of my parents and the geography of my birthplace. How does that "luck" allow me to default into heaven? What if I had been born a Hindu, believing in multiple gods, or a Muslim? What happened to all the people who lived before Jesus came on earth to save them? During this time of still wanting to believe in Jesus or at least some rendition of a prince of peace and love, my mind often drifted to the people in remote areas of the world who would never hear about Jesus. There would be no hope for those according to the Christian dogma since only through Jesus are people saved. That definitely had not made sense to me. How could a loving God not address this? And, I questioned, what about all other religions?

If I had been born in India, chances are I would believe in numerous gods, and in reincarnation. I wondered why reincarnation was not included in the Bible. Perhaps, early Christians could not include it with their beliefs because if they had many lifetimes to look forward to, they would have too many second and third chances. In retrospect, it seems clear that the threat of hell turned out to be much more effective at controlling the masses. I didn't have to thoroughly research every religion to find that God was made in man's image and not the other way around.

As for those who protest that I am robbing people of the great comfort and consolation they gain from Christianity, I can only say that Christianity includes hell, eternal torture for the vast majority of humanity, for most of your relatives and friends . . . If I could feel that I had robbed anybody of his faith in hell, I should not be ashamed or regretful.—Rupert Hughes, an American historian and novelist

Chapter 6

The Best Intentions with our Youth

> *[Children] are taught that it is a virtue to accept statements without adequate evidence, which leaves them a prey to quacks of every kind in later life, and makes it very difficult for them to accept the methods of thought which are successful in science.*—J.B.S. Haldane, biologist

I missed Santa when I no longer believed in him. I knew of him as a gift-giver who was jolly, kind and generous. He had a nice and a naughty list which worried me a little but I trusted that the nice side would always prevail. Besides, I didn't know anyone who hadn't received a Christmas gift. When I was a young girl, my dad succeeded rather easily at helping me prolong the wonderful delusion of Santa. On Christmas Eve every year, he locked our family dog in the barn so as not to scare the reindeer. Naturally, I wondered why would someone as serious and credible as my dad do such a thing if it wasn't completely necessary.

Then it happened. I was near the age of no longer believing but still hoping that it was true, and I heard it. I heard a bell that sounded (coincidentally) similar to the cow bells that our dairy cows wore. It was Christmas so I decided it must be Rudolph's bell, and it sounded like it was on our roof! That was it for me—it is true, I thought; there truly is a wonderful, jolly, generous white-haired man who comes once a year to give us gifts. I had been convinced, but only for one more year. After the "death" of Santa, I started to think about who had lied to me about him, and, if they lied about this, what else had they lied about? How could I ever trust them again?

I remember my disappointment when our youngest son, Ty, completely and utterly discounted the truth of Santa. While other children his age still believed without any doubt, he laughed at the absurdity of the whole sham. I felt sad because my youngest was leaving behind a childhood fairytale too soon. As a last ditch effort to get him to still believe, I tried coercion: "You won't get any presents if you don't believe." He called my bluff of course and challenged me to prove the jolly old man existed; my feeble attempt included, "You prove he doesn't!" At only four years old, he had decided that extraordinary claims deserved extraordinary evidence.

Believing in Santa is a harmless tradition. I happily deceived my children as I had been deceived. We often do as our parents did without question. Eventually they learn the truth about Santa. As religious parents, we feel obligated, also, to pass on religious messages to children. Our kids trust that we would not lie to them, that we know what is true, or that we at least looked further into ideas before passing beliefs along with our authority.

* * *

Around seven years later while attending a Catholic school and grumbling about religion homework, Ty was sitting quietly at the dining room table when he re-visited the Santa challenge. "Do you believe in God?" he asked me.

"Of course I do!" I said with conviction then. "Don't you?"

He said, "No, I don't. How do you know he's real?"

I was shocked that he didn't believe in God; why wouldn't he? Then, to my surprise, he wanted some details to qualify my conviction. I panicked. "Well, I just feel it. It's about having faith." There, that will keep him satisfied, I thought. But then came the hammer.

"Well, prove it then."

He wasn't being contrary or rude; if I believed so strongly in something, surely I must have some real proof to back it up. He required something more substantial than a feeling. Why couldn't he just follow along like most kids did at that age? Why did he have to ask a question that I couldn't answer with any kind of authority? I was on shaky ground; I was definitely not the all-knowing devout or wise mother like Olivia Walton from the TV show, *The Waltons*, or Ma Ingalls from *Little House on the Prairie*.

Parental Obligations for the Faithful

> ***The fear of eternal punishment is a wicked thing
> to inflict on a child.***—Christopher Hitchens

I must confess I never read the Bible with my children. I failed to impose, in any serious way, the religious beliefs of my upbringing. However, as a parent I understood the obligation to lead my children, or to at least influence them, toward religious belief. That, I believed, would increase the odds of them growing up to be good moral people of faith, and even more importantly, point them toward an afterlife in heaven. They were taught early on to accept death, to know that Great-Grandma had gone to heaven, and that she was in a better place because God took her home. I had not seen anything wrong with comforting a child in this way. Whether it was true or not, what mattered was lessening the pain of loss. Deceiving a child with a Santa-type fairytale seemed fine, but I was starting to feel that when a child is at an age of reason that it is time to gently share the rest of the story about death and dying—the scientific truth as we know it.

When Devin and Kara, my kids from my first marriage were six and eight years old, I began to date Murray, who was not at all religious. At the time I believed that he wasn't a totally lost soul, since he had been baptized Anglican. I knew that I could work with him on the belief front and maybe sway him from what I considered then to be "the dark side." It was more about just believing in God, not about being devoutly religious. As our relationship grew more serious, I remember a few occasions when Devin and Kara and I said a prayer at night, asking God to open their future step-dad's heart so that he would believe. We were worried about his soul. I was worried about marrying someone who was not a believer. One of my co-workers at that time, a fundamentalist Christian, counselled me against marrying a nonbeliever, reminding me about what the Bible had to say about this idea. Even when I explained to him that Murray was a kind, tender-hearted man who helped everyone, my co-worker said that none of that really mattered as much as him being a believer, and unless he experienced a conversion, we would be doomed as a couple.

I had already been through the unpleasant experience of divorce and really didn't want to make another mistake. But I am astounded as I look back over the past two decades as Murray contentedly, sometimes curiously, joined me and the kids in church. When we left the Catholic Church, he joined us on our mission to find another church. Regardless of whether he respected or understood my beliefs, he loved me enough to understand that this was something important to me. He never interfered as I tried to parent all three of our children as Catholic, then as Christian, then back in the Catholic Church. I don't think I would have been so patient if our roles had been reversed.

During that time, although I never nudged him to join me as Catholic, I suspect that he was relieved when I finally stopped going to church. His relief was compounded when I stopped feeling guilty about not going. He had joined me in having Ty dedicated in the Alliance Church and then again as I had him baptized in the Catholic Church. Even though we had been married in an evangelical church, he was supportive as we eventually had our marriage blessed in the Catholic Church. He didn't share his thoughts at these confusing times, and I have to laugh now as I recall how silly it all must have seemed to someone who had never been indoctrinated into this seemingly strange world of religion. It is a testament to his patience and tolerance.

There were many times that I imagined how difficult this change would have been with a religious partner. How would we have parented our children with different philosophies? Other than the guilt that I felt, parenting in a less-than-devout way was less difficult because Murray wasn't religious. I was able to be as religious or non-religious as I chose, and to teach our kids as much about religion or faith as I wanted. It probably helped that I never felt comfortable trying to force them to believe some of the extraordinary claims of religion—maybe because I had difficulty believing it myself. I also never felt comfortable suggesting that they love a God who they were also supposed to fear.

The Fear Factor

I attended a youth retreat early on in this discovery process. My mom had attended almost forty of them as a participant, a driver and a helper, and since her community was hosting one, I decided to join her with Ty. Since he was resistant to believing without evidence, I decided that a few days immersed in great Christian music and quiet reflection might move him closer to considering a conversion.

I had been to a retreat called a Search Weekend when I was in high school. We were dropped off at the Catholic high school, and as we were registering, our watches were taken away. I had looked around and noticed that the school windows were covered so that we couldn't see the time of day. It had all seemed quite exciting and mysterious at the time. We were kept up late at night, slept on the floor of classrooms and were woken up very early each morning to singing in the hallways. Looking back, it had been very cult-like, but as a teenager, I enjoyed the music and making friends, and never questioned the experience. The music ministry began daily sessions with upbeat music to get everyone engaged and energetic, and then late into the evenings, created a receptive state with more contemplative, meditative music.

I saw a similar type of manipulation decades later at this retreat with Ty. The windows of the school and the church remained uncovered and watches were not collected but the music and the contemplative process were very similar. Families are included in youth retreats these days and as the evening turns to night, through the ritual of listening to endless soft music, everyone has the opportunity to be in the presence of the consecrated host—the little round cracker that they believe is Jesus' actual body.

I registered and we found a seat in the church. The youth leader of this retreat is an amazing singer; the melodies in his music were beautiful, uplifting, and contemplative but the first song wasn't over when Ty whispered to me that Grandpa needed him to help with tables for lunch. He quietly slid out of the pew and happily spent the rest of the retreat as Grandpa's helper. I stayed mostly because I loved the music, but also because I was curious.

I listened with interest to the youth leader's personal stories of his faith journey that was filled with extraordinary stories of supernatural experiences or miracles, and examples of how God had blessed him abundantly. His talk on JOY had a profound but unexpected impact on me. He explained that JOY means Jesus, Others, then Yourself. Okay, I thought, I could still accept Jesus first, but before I could serve or take care of others, I knew through experience that I had to first take care of myself. This may sound selfish, but I had learned the importance of reframing "selfish" in this context. Think of the analogy of the oxygen masks in airplanes: the flight attendant instructs adults to put the mask on ourselves first so that we can properly assist our children with their masks.

I wrote a letter to the youth leader when I returned home. I wanted to share with him my perspective on his JOY talk, but even more important, that his message about a "God [who]will chew you up and spit you out!" was unnecessary and harmful to kids. At the time, I still saw myself as a believer, even though my faith was less about the *Catholic* God and more about a generic Father of unconditional love. I wanted him to know that instilling fear could be more harmful than helpful, and to ask if he really wanted to force kids to love a God that they are so strongly encouraged to fear. (After the fear-of-hell talk, we had joined in singing the beautiful comforting song called "Be Not Afraid.")

I received a kind response shortly after, merely thanking me for sharing my thoughts. The retreats continue, and no matter how beautiful or moving their music is, they reinforce fear and continue to coerce young people to believe the propaganda or face hell.

Confirmation

This sacrament of the Catholic Church became one of the crossroads of my transition. There are seven sacraments—baptism, confirmation, communion, reconciliation or confession, marriage, holy orders, and anointing of the sick or last rights. How ironic that a sacrament called confirmation, meant to confirm faith, resulted in further loss of faith. And, more irony, the nun organizing the several month process, was one of the high school nuns who had influenced me in such a positive way decades ago. According to the Catholic timeline, Ty was due to be confirmed in the Catholic faith. We read the notes from his Catholic school; we saw the schedule for the Monday night meetings and the schedule of Sunday masses that he was to attend for the next seven months.

Ty was very vocal about *not* getting confirmed. I was still partly hoping that he would just go along with it, because that is what is expected in the Catholic school community, but because of his involvement with hockey, we had been too busy and missed the first meeting. We also hadn't gone to Sunday mass, the first one that we were required to attend in this process. Even without the busy hockey season, we might not have been to church but I thought that if we could follow the rules for just a few months, get him confirmed, at least the Catholic guilt to comply could be satisfied.

It didn't work out that way. We didn't get to church or to the meetings and the nun started calling us at home. She called every few nights but we didn't answer the phone. I didn't know what to say. Ty said that he didn't want to be confirmed because he didn't believe in much of what the Church taught. He became more defiant the more I pushed. I couldn't continue; I couldn't force him to do something that he didn't agree with—especially since I was having my own serious doubts at that time. The whole point of confirmation is a renewal of baptismal vows when a person reaches an age where he or she can choose to renew the faith that began at baptism. He did not wish to do this. Completely coincidentally, we were invited for supper by our friend's uncle, the local bishop, a few days later. How was I to profess a faith via a religion that I had some fundamental problems with, and admit my inability as a Catholic parent to properly influence my son's spiritual growth?

I finally answered the phone when the nun called and arranged to meet her at the church the following day. It was so strange seeing her again after almost three decades. She sounded the same and actually looked the same, other than some subtle signs of aging. She was probably in her seventies.

It was at that point that I decided not to follow along because I was no longer convinced myself. I felt ready to take a stand with her, to stand between the Church and Ty, to protect him from the coercion of my childhood religion. Face-to-face, though, I caved. Despite my pep talk (to myself), I was unable to be assertive with the elderly nun. I politely agreed to do my best, to do what a good Catholic parent should do. But when we got home, it was back to hockey and our busy schedule without confirmation meetings or church obligations.

It was more than a year before I visited a church again. The service was for a celebration of confirmation, although not a Catholic one. I had actually been looking forward to attending. I love uplifting music so I thought that I could ignore the religious dogma. I enjoyed singing along with the first song but when the dynamic minister began talking, I was shocked. He referred to the young teenagers as "stains" and advised the congregation to continue to "fear the Lord." These young people were in the process of affirming their faith, so why focus on the fear factor at this point? Then I realized that the message was for the whole congregation! The minister reiterated that we were all nothing without Jesus, that we were also not even worthy of God's grace, and that we were born as unfortunate sinners.

My heart sank as he told the congregation how in need of grace we were. I looked around at the attentive faces nodding in agreement. My heart sank further as he introduced the reconciliation part of the service and repeated the reasons why the 13-year-old confirmands needed to be forgiven for their "sinful lives." It made me sad that this church leader was telling people how horrible they were as a way to convince them that they needed forgiving and saving. He reinforced how, without God's grace, we would go to hell. As I watched the beautiful pure little faces, I could not see them as stains, in need of saving from anything . . . except perhaps the deprecatory words of their minister.

Catholic Schools and our Kids

At 12 years old, Ty had arrived home from school one day to tell me that the teacher had told the students in health class that they would go to hell if they chose to wear a condom or use the birth control pill. As far as the Catholic Church is concerned, abstinence before marriage is the only appropriate option of birth control, but I wondered, do we have to use hell to ensure our kids choose to practice safer sex?

I spoke to a Catholic School Board member who confirmed that the message in school is supposed to be abstinence, period. I called the school and had a discussion with the teacher about the conversation in class. He confirmed the message of "abstinence only" but said that when the students had started asking questions, he tried his best to answer them. I felt sympathy for the teacher's dilemma and the challenge of teaching abstinence only, when the students legitimately question the illogical and harmful dogma. Unfortunately, the absence of reasonable answers has the possible consequence of lessening the credibility of the teachers.

Camp

One of the reasons that we had chosen a public school for Ty for grade eight the following year was to get a much-needed break from harmful Catholic dogma in the academic environment. He enjoyed a wonderful, unforgettable year at the public school, and I had been impressed by the extraordinary dedication of his teachers and the principal. Unfortunately, there had been one blip—during the final week of school.

Ty sent me a text after 10 o'clock the first night of the year-end camping trip. I was four hours away at a course for work. His text described the prayers lead by camp counsellors before each meal, the Christian music around the campfire, and the counsellors' stories about the supernatural and the occurrence of miracles. This might have been fine if we had sent him to a Christian camp, but we hadn't—not that we were aware of. He had been reprimanded when after the first prayer, he whispered to his friend, "Oh my God Russell!" The camp counsellor scolded, "We are courteous of God here!" The students heard about how they could be saved and one of the counsellors referred to the campers across the lake as the "crazies" then explained, "That's the Catholic Camp. We wouldn't want to go there!"

During the school year Ty's class had fundraised for this trip that had turned out to be a camp focussed on Christian evangelization. We were unaware, never thinking that a public school would participate in, or support, a religious camp. Fees for the camp not only funded the camp but also several evangelical churches a few hours away.

The 13-year-olds had been encouraged but not forced to participate in religious prayers and rituals differing from our family's beliefs. Even when the students were given the option to participate, there was undoubtedly a subtle but powerful pressure from peers and camp counsellors to join in so as not to be excluded from the group. If they were perceived as being reluctant to participate, they were reprimanded and then intimidated with the threat of extra duties.

The name of this evangelical camp had been changed decades earlier from a "Bible Camp" to Camp Kadesh. Its website claimed: "Being a place of decision for the children of Israel, better represented the original desire of having camp be a place of decision." As I read the information on the website, I realized how much my perspective had changed about religion. I could not respect the things that I was reading. The evangelical religion sounded strange, maybe even ridiculous, and I wondered how I could have once believed many of its Christian tenets. I was even more disappointed that young people are still regularly subjected to the propaganda at camp, often sent by unsuspecting parents. The camp's mission statement encourages churches to evangelize through camps, retreats and conferences. The Statement of Faith on the website includes adherence to the inerrant word of the Bible (the Old and New Testaments being inspired and commanded by God). The "fall" is described as Adam's disobedience of God, which resulted in the corruption of humans, and then the need for God's grace to save them from being condemned to hell.

I later discussed what happened at the camp with Ty's teacher and she confirmed that the school had rented

I Married an Atheist . . . thank God!

only the facility and the camp had agreed to avoid the usual proselytizing. But, there happened to be a new manager at the camp who chose to do otherwise, without parental or school permission. I remembered back to my own childhood as Christian prayer was imposed at an age when kids are intellectually and emotionally vulnerable; our minds filled with superstitious, magic stories and the terrifying consequences of not turning to Jesus.

*   *   *

Despite his experiences in Catholic school through grade seven, Ty decided to return to a Catholic high school for grade nine. This may seem like a strange choice, but he chose the school for the excellent volleyball program, not for his spiritual growth. I was familiar with, and impressed by, the high quality of education as our older kids had also attended this school. Here, Ty knew that he would be expected to attend the nearby cathedral for mass, religious services in the school, as well as a religion class every semester.

Early in the year, this time in a religion, not health class, the grade nine teacher relayed the familiar message, "You are not allowed to wear condoms or use birth control." At least he qualified the Catholic message with some common sense about safer sex in a city that is the chlamydia capital of our province, and our province, the HIV capital of Canada. What I didn't expect was that this same teacher would tell the kids that evolution was "just a theory" and that scientists were very close to proving the existence of the Adam and Eve who supposedly started the world's population. I'm not a biologist but I know that when the word "theory" is used as a scientific term, it means the best explanation for a set of facts only once it has been very well-established through the rigours of logic, observation and empirical evidence. Outside of the context of science, the word theory is just an idea, a hunch, a guess. Since grade ten is when the students learn sciences such as biology and geography, I fully expect that the following years will see science and reason prevail and that evolution will be understood for what it is—an observable phenomenon that is supported by significant scientific evidence. It is through the sciences that we understand our natural world.

But, as disappointing as it was, I wasn't surprised. I conceded that I had no right to complain about Ty's Catholic school enrolment because we had supported his choice of school for his reasons and were prepared that he would hear some religious doctrine. He is mature enough not to be affected by an hour of dogma per week. It's all just silly to him. I do hope that he has the courage to question the teacher's science behind the Adam-and-Eve claim, and the erroneous attempt to discount something as scientifically proven as evolution.

If I was still a praying person, I might pray that regardless of the school, we teach our kids to think for themselves, and how to think even more than what to think. I would pray that we teach them that science, reason and knowledge are virtuous, and to beware of extraordinary claims without credible evidence.

It is encouraging that there is support for adults like me who have struggled with childhood indoctrination. It's available through enlightening books, atheist blogs, and websites such as RichardDawkins.net, Freedom From Religion Foundation, Project Reason, The Friendly Atheist, and sites specifically for the ex-Mormon, ex-Islamist, ex-Catholic, ex-Jewish, or ex-fundamentalist Christian, and so on. My hope is that kids as well as adults will feel free to ask questions when things do not make logical sense. What I have found after taking it more seriously, is that little about religion does make sense.

The potential damage in imposing a Catholic school on our children was offset, I hope, by a non-religious home life. They succeeded, despite the limiting messages in school, in growing up to be independent thinkers, free from deception and irrational doctrine. They treat others well, not out of fear of hell or to gain reward in heaven, but because it is the right thing to do.

I am grateful that they will never suffer from Catholic guilt and they don't believe in hell. They are good people, follow the Golden Rule and respect others as well as themselves. The harm done to children in the name of religion is something that I will never accept. The only antidote for the anger is finding ways to speak up when the propaganda is overt and harmful or potentially life threatening, as it is in the message about condom use in Catholic schools. I will also speak up when Catholics and others attempt to minimize the impact of the systematic child rape at the hands of our trusted priests. I will not remain silent if I hear adults discouraging young people from thinking freely and critically about any ideas, especially beliefs that were once off limits to questions and criticism.

Imagine the people who believe such things and who are not ashamed to ignore, totally, all the patient findings of thinking minds through all the centuries since the Bible was written. And it is these ignorant people, the most uneducated, the most unimaginative, the most unthinking among us, who would make themselves the

> **guides and leaders of us all . . . I personally
> resent it bitterly.**—Isaac Asimov

*   *   *

My frustration grew as I became increasingly aware of how religion continues to be infused into all of our lives every day. I watched several disasters unfold in the media while working through the cognitive dissonance of my beliefs and world view. Again and again, I watched God being given credit for "small" miracles while Mother Nature was blamed for the deaths of tens of thousands, including children. Before this, I had been grateful for the miracles. It had never dawned on me that an omnipotent Father could have prevented the suffering if he chose to, and that there might not be a "divine" purpose to our suffering after all.

Chapter 7

Divine Disaster Relief

Live a good life. If there are gods & they are just, then they will not care how devout you have been, but will welcome you based on the virtues you have lived by. If there are gods, but unjust, then you should not want to worship them. If there are no gods, then you will be gone, but will have lived a noble life that will live on in the memories of your loved ones.—Marcus Aurelius

I have a young relative now in her twenties who has suffered with serious complications related to juvenile diabetes, initially diagnosed at four years old. She had been the cutest baby girl, the first grandchild for my parents. As she struggled immensely with this disease, particularly during the last four years, I thought about her daily. She was especially on my mind as I tried to understand or accept the suffering of human beings in the context of religion. She has been hospitalized for much of the time and all of the prayers that her family have mustered haven't seemed to make a difference in her condition. I have heard some theists explain suffering with the absurd idea that suffering is in some way a divine punishment. Some theists believe that there is something to learn from this torment, that we are not always supposed to know the reasons that God allows such horrific things to happen to his children. Perhaps he *had* intervened, or her condition would have been even worse. We were told that there is no greater love than a parent for a child, but what parent would do this to their children?

I used to worry about praying more, or harder, or differently. Maybe our prayers were not consistent with God's plan for her. If it is only the blessed that get to be healed, then how could we have her included on the "blessed list?" Could it be that she has a lesson to learn or maybe her family has a lesson to learn, as some theists might suggest?

Or, perhaps I just needed to accept that this brave and strong woman was born with a horrible disease. The best that we could do is to be there for her and her parents, with supportive words and assistance. Prayers might have been a kind gesture, and made *us* feel better, but they were futile as an actual end to her suffering. We are an animal species in a physical world, subject to illnesses and natural disasters. The world is often harsh, and terrible things happen in life, to us and our loved ones. These things are not the plan of a loving or punishing Father, or anybody's fault; they are just a very unfortunate part of life. I find it less disconcerting now to accept reality than to believe in a loving Father who can do anything, but chooses to do nothing to alleviate the pain and suffering of our loved ones.

As I left Catholicism and Christianity in general, I was starting to notice things that I had never noticed before. It now seemed ridiculous to see sports stars thanking God when they won, as if God was on their side. The sports teams, the celebrities accepting awards, the survivors of an accident believing that a higher being intervened on their behalf: I once thought that wearing one's faith on one's sleeve was such a humble tribute. Now I see very little humility when winners and survivors take opportunities to publicly acknowledge that they are favoured by a "Supreme Power." If God was to be given the credit for all the good, then I thought, he would also have to take credit for the atrocities such as health crises, accidents, and natural indiscriminate calamity.

"God never left us," proclaim the headlines when 33 Chilean miners were freed after being trapped for several days. I was curious why any God would allow the mine collapse in the first place. When someone eventually recovers from illness or injury due to the advancements of medicine and science, their tendency is to thank God for coming through for them, but who allowed the illness or accident in the first place? I questioned the whereabouts of God when tens of thousands were killed in the tsunami in Japan while I was writing this. Daily tragedies occur around the world where there is no sign of "divine intervention." God seemed to choose not to intervene. There was a time that I squared this with the concession that our meek, mortal minds lacked the capacity to understand his *wise* ways. I used to pray for people experiencing loss and difficult struggles, rather than asking why an omnipotent creator could not or would not stop natural or human tragedy. I accepted that God had a plan for me, for everyone. We were supposed to passively concede that it was just meant to be.

Shortly after the earthquake in Japan, where more than 8,000 were killed, thousands more missing and left homeless, and where the disaster was followed by the threat of a nuclear crisis, I read an article online called "Finding

Faith Amid Disaster".[19] It summed up what I now see as the hyperbole of faith as a source of comfort in times of suffering. The article includes several interviews of prominent authors and religious leaders from different faith backgrounds who attempt to answer this question after horrific disasters: "How could God let this happen?"

In *When Bad Things Happen to Good People*, author Rabbi Harold Kushner explains that these disasters are acts of nature not God; that God is with the people and provides the courage to continue on with their lives. He explains that God is in the generosity of the people as they help each other in times of tragedy. This made little sense to me as I watched the suffering that was shown on the news. God may have been in the courage of the people, but he was absent in using his omnipotence to stop the disaster. It bothers me how often Mother Nature gets the bad rap for so-called natural disasters, but when there is a lone survivor out of the thousands who died in the tragedy, God gets the credit for performing a miracle.

A Buddhist chief priest named Rev. Tesshu Shaku discussed the law of cause and effect from the perspective of a religion with no God. He described the earthquake as it was described in science and explained that for Buddhists, the focus was on relationships rather than faith: the result of a tragedy was often a change in perspective, a move toward being more spiritual and active in the community. I also once believed that God allowed disasters so people would come to him, so that they would become more spiritual.

---

[19]   Jessica Ravitz and Carol Costello "Finding Faith Amid Disaster", CNN March 20, 2011, accessed April 22, 2012. http://religion.blogs.cnn.com/2011/03/20/finding-faith-amid-disaster/).

Now I see that using the compassion and goodwill of others in a disaster, is just an awful way to entice someone to come closer. I do not believe that these people suffered an untimely death so that others would have the opportunity to become more spiritual. Many people actually lose their faith due to the lack of answers provided during times of tremendous suffering and loss.

The Rev. James Martin, a Jesuit priest, conceded that there was no adequate answer to explain the reasons for suffering. We should instead be comforted by the belief that God suffers along with us, and that he is no stranger to suffering after he suffered with Jesus on the cross. He too, talked about how people could become more religious during these times: "when our defences are down and we're more vulnerable, God can break into our lives more easily." To me, this sounded coercive and unkind—like he sits idly by until we are at our lowest.

The idea of God suffering along with us is not at all comforting when I think of children dying in their parents' arms. I feel that it would be a cruel intention to allow suffering so that he could join us in the experience.

Dr. Sayyid Syeed, national director of the Islamic Society of North America's Office of Interfaith and Community Alliances, answered the question by first clarifying that disasters are not a consequence of our sins. He described tragedy as a test from God and said that God tests those that he loves. I had to wonder, what happens to his children that he doesn't love.

Sam Harris, the author of *The End of Faith* and *Letter to a Christian Nation*, offered a compassionate response from a secular viewpoint. He explained simply that terrible things happen to innocent people. He also explained how compassion fades with the religious ideas that disasters are part of God's plan, that they are just meant to be, or that people somehow get what they deserve.

As I was editing this chapter I was watching a documentary about the 2004 tsunami that killed 227,073 people, of which likely one-third were children. The dead and missing were from across 12 countries. Actual video footage depicted parents and children clinging to each other, and their devastation and despair as they could hang on no longer. They must have found it difficult to trust an almighty being that did nothing though had the capacity for "miracles." It became impossible for me to accept that these victims of natural disasters would believe that God hadn't forgotten them.

Understanding the Rationalizations

I always wondered how prayer really worked. When I was little, my prayer had been the "Now I lay me down to sleep" one, and as an adult, it had changed to "Thank you God for everything that you have given me. Please give food to those who don't have any. Amen." It became such a habit that I still catch myself saying it from time to time as I drift off. I thought if I prayed and nothing happened, it was because I might not have realized how he actually answered my prayer. But, if he really knew my heart and what was best for me, what was the point of asking in the first place, especially if he was going to do what he planned anyway? If he did answer in an agreeable way, it was because I'd been the recipient of his blessing. Sometimes, I was told, his answer was to wait for the answer. I have since realized that other than providing us with something to do when feeling helpless in very difficult times, prayer does little else.

Credible studies on prayer have been done over the years and science has proven that God does not answer prayers on earth: "No matter how many people pray. No matter how sincere those people are. No matter how much they believe. No matter how devout and deserving the recipient. Nothing will happen. The legs will not regenerate. Prayer does not restore the severed limbs of amputees."[20] Even considering all the miracles that have supposedly occurred, there has been no evidence of God ever growing a limb back for an amputee. Also, "Every single 'answered prayer' is nothing more than a coincidence . . . The fact is, believers who pray die from this disease [cancer] at exactly the same rate as people who do not."[21]

A 2006 article in the *New York Times* by Raymond J. Lawrence outlined a $2.4 million study by Dr. Herbert Benson, cardiologist and director of the Mind/Body Medicine Institute near Boston. The scientific study showed that intercessory prayer is not medically effective. Even less promising, the people who were told that they were being prayed for fared worse than the people that were told only that there might be others praying for them.[22]

*   *   *

[20] http://whywontgodhealamputees.com/god5.htm, accessed May 6, 2012.

[21] http://godisimaginary.com/i2.htm, accessed May 6, 2012

[22] Raymond J. Lawrence, "Faith-Based Medicine" Opinion, *New York Times,* April 11, 2006, accessed May 6, 2012. http://www.nytimes.com/2006/04/11/opinion/11lawrence.html?_r=1&ex=1302408000&en=643ff6eac0f51086&ei=5088&partner=rssnyt&emc=rss

I was finally finished with faith—the kind in religion anyway. It was time to expand my search outside of religion. This part of my experience took me to a strange but interesting new world. Within it, I worked through much anger, not just about the imposition of religion in our lives or the atrocities of the Catholic Church, but also about being duped from a young age. I was angry at myself for wasting so much time, for not being courageous enough to inquire earlier in my life. The reward came only when I gave myself permission. I was amazed at the number of people I found who no longer had an interest in religion.

At this time, I was still strangely left with an idea of an impersonal God, or some power that created the universe. And, even if the vengeful, judgmental, jealous, loving God of the Bible no longer made sense, there still had to be something out there to believe in. I had to find out if we were just spinning in the universe without some higher purpose for being here. Now that I was truly free to look outside of religion, what I found was extraordinary!

Chapter 8

The Possibilities

I have recently been examining all the known superstitions of the world, and do not find in our particular superstition (Christianity) one redeeming feature. They are all alike, founded upon fables and mythologies.—Thomas Jefferson

Have you ever had an experience that seemed so coincidental that it must have been part of a larger plan? A particular dramatic one of mine comes to mind: I was getting ready to climb down a ladder from the second floor of our new house that was under construction. As I had done numerous times, I lifted our then three-year-old son Ty onto my back to take him down with me. As we moved closer to the ladder that leaned against the frame where the stairs would be built, something told me to put him down and climb down the ladder without him. I heeded that little voice, put Ty down and proceeded to climb onto the ladder. The next thing I knew, I was lying on my back on the cold concrete floor, with the ladder underneath me. I could feel intense pain in my foot and I could see blood flowing down my arm from my elbow. I had pain in my wrists from swinging my arms trying to grab on to the ledge while I was falling. The ladder had slid on the new concrete. Murray and Ty were stuck up on the second floor without a way down to assist me. With no one else around to help, I managed to hop up on the foot that wasn't injured, drag the ladder a few feet and reach it up to Murray. We drove to the emergency room where x-rays were taken and my injuries were treated. I spent some time at home healing and resting and eventually recovered from the injuries.

As terrifying as it was to fall nine feet, it was more upsetting to relive the moments with Ty still on my back before the fall. What if I hadn't listened to that little voice in my head? If I'd had Ty on my back when I fell he could have been injured very badly or even killed. What is that little voice in our heads that warns us about danger, or the intuition or sixth sense that causes the person that you were just thinking about to telephone?

Even though I have trouble remembering what I did yesterday, I have an uncanny (my family calls it "weird") sense of where to find lost objects at home. It may be due to the fact that we build houses and move every few years so objects in our house are never too far from memory, but no one else can ever seem to find anything like I do. I just concentrate on seeing the object and before long, its whereabouts is pictured quite clearly in my mind. My family jokes about my new age "psychic" abilities and has learnt that rather than wasting time looking, they just ask me to use my special powers.

By this time I had already experienced the apprehension of letting go of my religion, but now I was surprised to discover a belief system that included an afterlife without hell. It also included explanations about my intuitiveness or sixth sense. These believers sometimes call themselves

Spiritualists, sometimes New Agers, but their common idea is that God is inside each of us, and that we are all connected to this common source. Rather than "God," some call this "Source," some call it "Universe," and some call it "All That Is." They believe that divinity, beauty, grace and guidance are all within, and our souls can recycle back to earth for many lives. It sounded so nice; I was beginning to enjoy exploring.

I liked the idea that there wasn't anything that we could do to get rid of our life source. It could never be snuffed out. I liked that it was described as something that connects us all: the emotions that we feel as we love our children, and as we connect in meaningful ways to other human beings. Source, Universe, All That Is seemed similar to my idea of heaven but without a Supreme Being to worship and to fear. As I had only recently peeled away the layers of religion, this new idea didn't yet make sense to me but I thought it was worth further investigation.

It started with the television show *Medium*, loosely based on a real-life psychic, also known as a medium. Alyson Dubois was a woman who, sometimes successfully, assisted police in finding missing people. I had watched *Medium* for a few years and thought that the story behind it was quite fascinating. I considered at that time that this medium must be gifted—the real deal—based on some evidence of successful outcomes in the cases that she was involved in. I wanted to learn more.

Secret Learning from Sylvia Browne

If people like the real Alyson Dubois did have psychic abilities, maybe there was also some truth to what famous psychics like Sylvia Browne claim to do. I was shopping for groceries one day and as usual, I was unable to pass a book aisle without a quick look. The particular book that caught my eye on this occasion was called *The Mystical Life of Jesus—An Uncommon Perspective on the Life of Christ.* Even though the book was written by Sylvia Browne, the psychic, it was about Jesus and Christianity. With some lingering residue of Catholic guilt, I justified that I was really just reading about Jesus. Spending money and time on a psychic would have been considered a sin in my past.

This was the first time outside of the Church that I really considered some of the possibilities outside of natural phenomena, of the "supernatural." I didn't know much about mediums but I had seen a card reader a couple of times out of curiosity and for entertainment, years ago. Of course, I had felt compelled to attend the confessional soon after each occasion!

Reading Browne's book over a few days, I enjoyed a new perspective on why we're here, how we are all connected, and how what really matters in the end is compassion and how we treat each other. This really didn't sound evil; why would the Church forbid us to read about values similar to Christian ones? The *biggie* of sinful religious messages in the book had to do with reincarnation. Browne's belief is that the soul continues on, like a flicker of light that never goes out. We complete a stint on earth, return home, and then prepare for another incarnation. The word reincarnation still made me react, but I read on.

In fact, I read several of Sylvia Browne's books and I was intrigued at how much information she was able to receive from "the other side." Her "spirit guide" had been with her since she was a young girl. How nice it would be to have a guide who would answer all questions regarding life, death, the hereafter, and the existence of a soul, I thought. And I could imagine everyone going to the same place after we die—without hell as an option! I loved the idea that when we die, our soul reunites with a universal source where the next adventure or life is decided. This idea was—no Satan, no hell, and no real death. This was a belief system I could consider, so that I could truly enjoy my life free from the dread of death.

I find it strange even now as I write these words. This was such an unlikely source in which to find comfort—and more comfort, I realized, than I had found in religion. My poor mom probably felt like her only daughter had been caught in the vortex of what she called "that New Age crap." I had tried to share the great news I had about hell and Jesus' married life but she went into the laundry room and didn't come out for a while. I had so much information for her to consider: that we do not have to worry about hell, that we no longer have to earn our way to heaven or to win God's favour, that we are not born as sinners, and that God doesn't punish. But she was not pleased with my new-found insights and looked at me as if I had grown two heads. I knew then that this was a topic that we would avoid in the future.

The idea that there was no such thing as "death" was such a relief to me, however. What was left to be afraid of? I could hope that we would all end up in the same place at the end of this lifetime and maybe death would just be the revolving door to another exquisite experience on earth.

In her book, *The Mystical Life of Jesus—An Uncommon Perspective on the Life of Christ*, Sylvia Browne claims to know things that I had never heard before: the Dead Sea Scrolls had been found in 1947; Jesus had learned about healing, meditation and Eastern Philosophy, and while the

Essenes saw baptism as washing away all past life trauma, Christianity had turned it into the concept of cleansing of original sin. Browne also claims that the Adam and Eve story was meant to be symbolic, and that the timelines in the New Testament are inconsistent so the Bible can't always be relied on as an absolute text. She claims that God is all loving and merciful; his love is perfect and there is no judgment day or punishing of the wicked.

I was also intrigued by Sylvia Browne's more honourable depiction of Mary Magdalene. This was the first time that I thought about Mary Magdalene since reading *The DaVinci Code* by Dan Brown and was introduced to the idea that she was more than a friend of Jesus. I also hadn't known that a Gospel of Mary existed; it had apparently surfaced in Egypt in 1896. Mary's gospel was never included in the Bible. The more I read about Mary, the more interested I became in her life—the not-so-shiny-version that I had heard growing up, then this other life that depicted a strong, wealthy woman who had been Jesus' partner, support, and confidant.

I thought back to the years when I was trying out different Catholic churches in the city, and a friend had recommended a small parish on the far end of town. She said that there was a fundraising auction planned for the following Sunday, which included the priest's wonderful paintings. I attended the mass and enjoyed the sermon about grace, forgiveness and the unconditional love of Jesus. Still a believer, albeit a weak one, I was making an effort to strengthen my faith but was entrenched in feelings of guilt and insecurity. The priest's words had been comforting to me. After mass, I walked to the area of the auction items and was impressed by the quality of the priest's paintings. One picture in particular caught my attention—a very beautiful picture of Mary Magdalene. She did not look at all like the prostitute that, until recently, the Church had depicted her as.

As I walked around the area of the fundraiser, two different people approached me and pointed out my resemblance to Mary Magdalene in the painting. The hair stood up on the back of my neck. Later my friend who had recommended this parish also asked if I had noticed my resemblance to Mary. Soon after, I read a book called *The Mary Magdalene Within* about Mary's love story with Jesus, written by Joan Norton. After her teenage daughter had died in a car accident, Norton spent years trying to connect with the spirit of her daughter through meditation. One early morning as she was meditating, it wasn't her daughter but Mary Magdalene who came through, asking that she share Mary's love story with the world. The short story was written in Mary's words and showed a very different side to this *companion* of Jesus.

I loved this new idea of honouring the feminine side of humanity, especially via the possibility that Mary's strong voice may have been given to women at a time when women had no authority in most societies. My own strength and voice as a woman were initially stirred by an entertaining novel of Dan Brown's, then by the strange connection with a priest's painting, and now by the warmth of Mary's beautiful love story. Somehow, having Mary Magdalene in my life invoked a feeling of empowerment. I had been aware of women's oppression and mistreatment throughout history but never considered how these attitudes continue today—not just in Muslim countries but in the western world as well. I didn't see myself as an oppressed woman, but I felt deeply connected to the suffering of women and the ongoing inequality. Suddenly I felt different as a woman—relevant and open to new perspectives.

It didn't matter if it was true or not; I loved thinking about Mary Magdalene as an advocate for equality and respect for woman during her time on earth. Her gospel has her playing a more prominent role—at the very centre of the Jesus movement. Had women taken a more active role in the Christian Church not even two years after Jesus' death? Did the "prostitute" of the Catholic Church actually help to teach the men at that time?

Whether I believed Sylvia Browne and the messages that her lifelong spirit guide shared with her or not, I would no longer see mediums or psychics as evil. Reconciling her belief in Christ, alongside her "sinful" gift of mediumship, in a strange or ironic way, made a safe platform for me to step out onto initially. Sylvia turned out to be just the beginning.

Spiritual, Not Religious

> *A multitude of aspects of the natural world that were considered miraculous only a few generations ago are now thoroughly understood in terms of physics and chemistry.*—Carl Sagan

After reading Sylvia Browne, I couldn't believe how many "professional" mediums existed. I had gone to the library and found a larger-than-expected section on the supernatural, especially on the many gifts that people seem to possess to communicate with the dead. I became aware of a huge movement believing in a Universal Soul, in channelling, crystal healing energy, and different realms of existence beyond our three dimensions. Apparently, this is how mediums see things and hear things that others cannot:

they are more sensitive to these other "less-dense" realms of existence where souls move after death. People, who are open to, or sensitive to this realm, can communicate with others who have "crossed over" from the third dimension. How fascinating, I thought at the time. Perhaps this is how I am able to locate lost objects with my mind's eye . . .

I was starting to see that religious people could be spiritual, but spiritual people do not require the man-made dogma of religion. Spirituality is not exclusive or divisive; it is not religion. It is personal. People who no longer accept the tenets of any religion but still believe in a spiritual realm refer to themselves as simply spiritual.

Finally, what a relief to think instead that we could all be going to the same place and that life may have been predetermined! The books that I was reading at that time about past lives suggested that before we were born, we decided challenges we wanted to experience, and lessons we wanted to learn during this lifetime. What if I had decided what kind of life I was going to have this time around, before I was born: who my parents would be, my husband, my children, and what career I would have?

I considered this idea with interest for several months and for this brief period viewed my life and family differently, as living out a secret contract that none of us were really aware of. It was interesting also to view death as predetermined. Imagine dealing with the loss of a loved one knowing that together you had pre-planned the time and type of death, and would be together again in the afterlife to plan another life and death together.

Reading about ancient spiritual mysteries of the world was refreshing and interesting. I read and watched videos about the Spiritualists and New Age, crystal healing, angel therapy, Shamanism, past life regression, near death experiences, other types of mediums, such as channels, about perhaps a more accurate depiction of Mary Magdalene, and the Divine Feminine. I read books by atheists, agnostics and humanists, and thoroughly enjoyed Bill Maher's comedic but poignant inquiry about religion called *Religulous*.

I enjoyed a book called *The Pagan Christ: Recovering the Lost Light* by Tom Harpur, on a magnificent stretch of white sand beach in the Mayan Riviera, Mexico, about a man named Horus in ancient Egypt, who was born of a virgin and was considered to be the Christ of Egypt, long before Jesus. He'd had a supernatural birth on December 25th and was a fisher of men with twelve followers. This mythology dates back to 2000 BCE. The birth of the Persian sun god Mithras was also said to have occurred between 3000 and 2400 BCE on December 25. His story is similar, right down to several miracles, his death and resurrection.

I have looked into both ends of the spectrum trying to understand fanatics and non-believers. The different major religions fascinated me but as I read, I felt impatience toward any belief system that preached that its way is the only way, perpetuating division, judgment, intolerance and even hatred. The dozens of books that found their way to my eager fingertips opened my mind to many perspectives, some more strange than interesting. My plan was to study without judgment (especially of myself) and see where that took me, to see what ideas resonated as I read, and to consider all possibilities. What is the truth, based on the most current empirical scientific evidence?

I had been at a management workshop years ago when the facilitator mentioned a film that makes an attempt to help us to realize our potential as human beings, to receive whatever we desire in life and to be successful and happy in whatever we choose to do. The film was called

What the Bleep Do We Know? with hearing-impaired actor Marlee Matlin. About a year later I finally watched it and it helped me see spirituality differently. I was able to re-frame "spiritual" without muddying the concept with religion. It did, however, further muddy the critical difference between science and religion, which is discussed further in the final chapters.

Deepak Chopra's book *Life After Death* dropped into my hands at the airport as I was perusing the book section for a book for my flight. It took only a few days to read and I loved mostly how it further solidified Satan and hell as a delusion. Chopra proposes the concept of God as existing inside of us, claims death is an illusion and discusses the circumstances under which the soul is revealed to people in their lives. I was able to follow his ideas until chapters swerved into what intellectual critics of his work refer to as "woo." At first I regarded him as credible because he is a scientist not a theologian, but after considering a number of his books, I found him a little too bizarre.

Soon afterward, I read several books written by a psychiatrist named Brian Weiss, who had been doing his regular therapy with a patient using hypnosis to assist possible recollections of childhood trauma, when something unexplainable happened: she went further back than her childhood and began to describe a past life! Through his practice Weiss now assists people in learning about past lives. This sounded quite convincing from someone with a PhD in psychiatry.

After reading some very entertaining books on past-life regression, I heard about an author named Paul Elder, a former mayor of a city in my province, who wrote a book about his several near-death experiences: *Eyes of an Angel.* He'd had three such experiences and communicated regularly with his spirit guide. His story was very interesting and somewhat convincing so I decided that it was time to take a break from the books and usual research, and make contact with my own spirit guide, to finally get some answers to lingering questions.

As I researched the practice of meditation, I learned about crystals. There was a long list of health benefits—everything from mental health to physical health, from stomach problems to depression—and I spent the next few months admiring the beautiful colours, shapes and possibilities of different remedies from semi-precious stones like rose quartz, hematite, and white howlite. What if these stones were a source of healing energy from the earth? I learned that the crystals that could benefit my own health and well-being would most likely be an inexpensive set that would assist in opening up my chakra system—the energy centres of the body. How could people make a living selling crystals if there wasn't some undeniable evidence that they worked? I bought a wonderful collection of semi-precious stones and followed the instruction book—which was more like a textbook—on how to clean and activate the crystals for optimal effectiveness. The book suggested that I would probably benefit after all of these years of never activating the energy centres in my body. I wondered how I had been able to function at all with closed chakras for so many years!

I wanted to continue to be healthy. I read instructions on how to use the crystals during meditation to clear and open these energy centers. It felt strange because, although I'm an advocate for stress reduction techniques like relaxation exercises, I had never actually tried any serious meditation. I took some time to get prepared. I set up a meditation room, which my family jokingly referred to as the room where I killed and sacrificed chickens. I began my first attempt at a meditation exercise. I slowed my breathing as instructed and felt my body begin to relax. Quieting my mind was another story. My mind wandered, I became bored, and not too long afterward, drifted off to sleep, which I probably needed more than anything.

The books said that meditation takes practice so I persevered for several months; every once in a while, in a quiet house, with the telephone ringer on mute, I would prepare myself and my room to venture into this realm. I was open to connecting and finding answers via my soul and the spirit world—should anyone choose to visit.

I did love the crystals. Focusing on shiny things was enjoyable, but despite a good effort, I never felt the earth move or even tremble, and I was never sure if my chakras were cleared or if they were ever open. I did enjoy providing my body and mind great moments of relaxation, but overall, felt no significant change in my physical or mental state that I could say was a result of crystal energy. Despite taking it seriously for some time, I never did hear from my spirit guide—maybe because I wasn't doing something quite right, maybe because my chakras were all plugged up, or maybe because it just isn't real. The books had said that there was no scientific evidence that crystals actually do anything and despite my desire to believe, my experience confirmed that they did nothing for me.

Travelling home from a ski trip in the mountains, I finished reading a book called *Conversations With God* by Neale Donald Walsch. This was an amazing "true" story of a man who was down and out in his life and after a plea for answers from God (to questions not unlike my own), a force literally took over his pen and started answering all of his questions. I loved the idea that God himself answered every question about life, death, sin, sex, money, fear, and extraterrestrials. So far my spirit guide hadn't come through for me so maybe this could be a way to find answers? Walsch's three volumes helpfully answered most of my questions but throughout my reading, as happy as I was for his good fortune, I had the recurring nagging feeling: why him? Why was Neale Donald Walsch so special that God had chosen to answer through him? What had made this supernatural experience available to him? I wasn't so much jealous as once again sceptical of the seeming randomness. Who gets picked and why?

Walsch's writings about God describe a much different God than that of the Bible. As the five attitudes of God, he lists joyful, loving, accepting, blessing and grateful. I could like this God who claims that in his reality, we are born pure God, Goddess, and pure Love and that we convince ourselves erroneously that everything that we humanly desire is bad—sex, love, joy, money, power. Walsch's book claims that the same destination after death awaits everyone. What I liked about these messages was the non-judgmental, non-religious way of looking at death and life. I liked viewing spirituality or some type of faith as an opportunity, not an obligation. I liked the message that we are not inherently sinners, and that God would not create less-than-perfect human beings then demand perfection or strike them with eternal damnation.

I took stock at this juncture of my inquiry into belief systems. So far, I had felt nothing with the crystals (perhaps their energy was too subtle for me) and despite purchasing the special meditation CD's, had no luck with out-of-body experiences, or hearing even one whisper of encouragement from my spirit guide. Maybe I just wasn't worthy, or doing something not quite correctly because some of it was quite complicated. Or maybe it, like the personal God of the Bible, just wasn't real.

But, I decided to give the esoteric one last try when an opportunity arose to attend Channelling Training in a nearby city. For an additional 300 dollars, I could even spend a private hour with the gifted channel (medium) and ask any questions I wanted.

Meeting with Mother Earth

I felt a little mischievous thinking about the unlikelihood that this meeting would have occurred a few years earlier. The session began after a short chat and lasted about 45 minutes. With my list of questions ready, I sat quietly as Pepper Lewis, the medium who channels Mother Earth or Gaia, as she's often called, closed her eyes and slowed her breathing. Gaia began speaking through the medium with an odd accent suggestive of medieval English. She sounded maternal and nurturing and called me things like "sweet one," or "my sweet." I liked her.

Gaia started with a short lesson on clearing the mind and being open to direction and discovery, and then she invited my questions. When I asked if she thought that I was going in the right direction in my life so far, she confirmed that I was. Since I had read several books about reincarnation and past lives, I was curious about my own previous times on earth. She explained the Crusades and the part that I played in them; I was excited at first to hear how I had fought for a cause during at least one lifetime. Then she described in more detail how I had been on the less-honourable side and how I'd responded when I realized (too late) that I had made a horrible mess, costing the lives of many. She told me how I'd had to sneak away in the middle of the night to the Greek islands.

Gaia described most of my previous lifetimes as struggles from quiet to more intense ways of living. I had once been a renegade who didn't fight the "good fight." I had to hide away again, change my appearance, and find a simpler life. There seemed to be a theme developing of me joining a group to fight a cause, only to realize later that it wasn't the right thing to do. She became quite animated when telling me about how I lived in hiding over several lifetimes and even when I had chosen the "good fight," I would not speak up because of the significant blunders in other lifetimes, and the grave danger in the past, in doing so.

We talked about the price we pay for talking about controversial ideas like those evolving out of religion and she promised that the price would be small. She explained that the price would be greater if I chose not to speak. I thought back to many times in my current life that I chose not to speak up, for fear of what others might think of me.

I had been journaling at the time, and wasn't yet sure about writing a book so I asked her about it. She suggested that a book would help me to sort my ideas and find some answers to the questions that I had. It would also be a way of speaking up and sharing my ideas. She confirmed that my path for this lifetime, now that I had learned how to empower myself, was to help others to empower themselves.

I asked Gaia about Mary Magdalene, who had somehow inspired courage in me to regard my femininity as a source of strength rather than the reason for remaining silent at times in my life. She talked about my "kinship" with Mary in other lives as well.

I had allowed myself to be victimized at times when I chose not to speak up and now this internal struggle seemed to be over. My insecurity and feeling of inferiority as a woman might have been the result of trying to find my way as a young girl growing up in the middle of six male siblings. I was often regarded differently than the boys and my young mind interpreted "different" as less significant in some way. Whether the experience was based on something real or not, I found the channel's words inspiring and worth considering.

I couldn't leave without asking about Murray. Gaia confirmed that Murray and I had indeed been together before this life. He was the lover who had helped me to sneak away in the middle of the night when I was making such a mess of things during the Crusades. Without even knowing anything about what I was really up to, he had protected me and stayed with me because of his love for me.

When I asked about our youngest son Ty, she spoke at length about his search for the truth and how he would not simply accept anything that he was told. I laughed as she accurately described a young teenager who is quick to discount ideas in which he finds fallacy. He has always been righteous—to a painful degree—and has never had patience for injustices. When he was eight years old, his grade two teacher had told us that he fought incessantly for other students if he believed that they'd been treated poorly by other students.

Our older son Devin had apparently been a monk in a previous life, and I had to laugh at that as well, because he has a calm, respectful personality that would have been well-suited to monastic life. My laughter bubbled over as the medium described our daughter Kara, and my relationship with her. In a past life together, we had both been queens of rather small, insignificant fiefdoms. We were known to fight over the silliest things such as pieces of pork. My laughter faded as Gaia emphasized how much smarter she is than me.

The session came to a close with some advice about how to take better care of my body and how as a great wise being, I could use my wisdom to attain optimal health and well-being in my life.

*   *   *

I left the hotel room thinking about whether any of the experience with the channel could be real or at all possible. I listened several times to the tape and wondered about past lives and what they meant, if true. What if there is a part of us that really does live on, not in the religious sense of heaven and hell, but as connected tiny units of energy. The medium had been convincing and somehow soothing. She shared an interesting perspective and my desire to consider it lasted for several months. I read books on shamans, on other types of mediums and again tried to see life—and death—from different perspectives. Kara and I laughed about our past life together as queens and pictured ourselves fighting over pieces of pork. She joked about being much cleverer and wittier than me, just as she knew all along!

As fascinating as this was, it was the only highlight of the weekend of Channelling Training. I had been very uncomfortable in the room full of people channelling and speaking on behalf of beings including dolphins, and entities from other places in the universe, and I must admit that I wasn't convinced that it was all real. I tried not to judge the authenticity of others' experiences but I was unsuccessful in connecting with anything unseen. This lack of success was sadly consistent with my valiant attempts to contact my spirit guide, who Gaia had told me was with me that weekend.

But, I did understand the attraction to the idea of "no real death." I would be extremely relieved if this belief system somehow, was empirically proven, but I have serious doubts. It was an enjoyable belief system to wade in for a while; I decided to make a note to return in my next life as a woman again, but one with a waist!

The End of a Fairytale

Learning about spiritualists and the New Age world was my favourite part of the journey to disbelief. Most of the once-religious people I spoke to denied being religious but were reluctant to admit that they didn't believe in things outside of the natural world. I understood the reluctance and for a time during my transition, saying that I was "just spiritual" was a safe default position, living within a religious culture. As I learned about being just spiritual, I learned how to relax my body and my mind and how to take some necessary time out, without feeling guilty about it. Ultimately, I could enjoy the idea of no hell, and the possible alternative, a place for us all to meet after this earthly life and prepare for another. I loved the crystals and the possibility that different realms exist. I also enjoyed the idea that there might be more lives after this life, and that I would plan these subsequent times on earth. How creative and exciting! Perhaps I was exactly where I was meant to be at this stage in my life. If everything was predetermined—my decisions, the good and the not so good, the path that I chose, the husbands, the children and the challenges that

I've lived through—I could feel less responsible for the not-so-good, accepting that it was all inevitable, all planned even before I was born.

The problem, though, was the lack of sufficient evidence for any of it. Despite my best efforts I failed to meet my spirit guide during that weekend (or ever), and I failed to channel the energy or wisdom of any sacred ancient beings. Regardless, it had been an effective way to thoroughly rid myself of the religious. Moving toward the spiritual had been very interesting, but I found the word "spiritual" very abstract and confusing, as it can cover everything from mysticism to higher power to immortal souls. We also use it when we talk about emotional and psychological well-being. Sometimes it's a way to sneakily impose religion.

Becoming spiritual not religious was an essential transition place for me, and helped my acceptance of death without the fear of hell. Quitting faith cold turkey would have been too difficult, especially after four decades of being Catholic. So what now? Having the *desire* to believe was not enough. With no evidence for religious claims, no evidence for the supernatural, what was left? Nothing . . . but also everything, because of how I became more truly free to live this life.

> *I regard the brain as a computer which will stop working when its components fail. There is no heaven or afterlife for broken down computers; that is a fairy story for people afraid of the dark.*—Stephen Hawking

Chapter 9

Finding Peace

It ain't the parts of the Bible that I can't understand that bother me, it's the parts that I do understand.—Mark Twain

I attended a number of funerals during the writing of this book and heard many phrases of consolation offered from well-meaning people: "God called him home," or "We are not meant to know his greater plan for our lives," or "God's compassion ended their suffering," or that "they are in a better place." If the God of the Bible did exist, he deserved some well-placed anger from shocked and grieving family and friends. Despite a desire to still believe at that time, I was finding no comfort at all in religion.

At one funeral, the priest asked some great questions, similar to my own. How could something so tragic happen? How could a loving Father take our loved ones this way? Where is the comfort for family and friends that are left behind with such immense grief? How can God's plan result in so much pain?

I am, and always will be, open to answers that make sense, especially to questions about tragedy and death. As

107

the priest listed his questions, I held my breath. Maybe he would have answers that could satisfy that part of me that still naturally wanted to make sense of something so horrible.

He had nothing. He admitted that there were no answers; that there is only grief. Trying to come to terms with his own feelings of grief and loss, this church leader, who conceded that there is no satisfactory reason for such a tragedy, had my admiration. But I was left empty. Even so, I appreciated that he did not default to the usual platitudes.

With life, naturally and unfortunately, comes death. "It's God's plan," falls short of satisfying and I was reminded again that a God of love would never cause this much pain: for our benefit or for a life lesson. Who would use death to teach us a lesson, or worse to prove that a suffering death can somehow be a sign of God's compassion? Accepting that this is a tragic end is difficult, but much easier than trying to understand or accept how a loving Father could be so cruel. But we're then told: as mortal humans, how could we expect to understand his immense plan for us? Yes, we are mortal, but that's the point, the only point.

I accept this now and expect no comfort in religion where death is concerned. To avoid the inevitable finality of my life and the lives of loved ones, I had wanted to believe that this life was not the end; that we are possibly reincarnated after death. True or not, I did understand the attraction of this part of religion and probably one of the main reasons for its longevity. But, not everyone seemed to need this comfort.

A Small Voice of Reason

During a discussion about death, my then 13-year-old Ty was claiming to know all the answers about the afterlife, so I asked him, "What do you think will happen when I die?"

"You're dead."

"Doesn't that make you sad?"

"It will, but that's life," he said matter-of-factly.

"Wouldn't you prefer to believe that I'm hovering around close to you, watching over you from heaven?"

"No, that's just creepy!" he said.

My husband and kids now know that any discussion of God at my funeral would be only for the sake of theists in attendance. I suspect that, especially after they know about my coming out as nonreligious, that some might pray for my soul in the faint hope that their gesture—heartfelt and not meant as judgment—will save me from a fiery eternity. Although it's generally a favourite for families of the deceased, I would prefer not to have "Amazing Grace" sung. I agree that the melody of this hymn is beautiful and one of the most touching, especially played by bagpipes. But, the words are not: the writer of the song describes himself struggling through a life of challenges. He refers to himself as a wretch and "blinded." He saves *himself*, however, because *he* makes significant changes. Sadly he chooses not to take credit and responsibility for his personal strength in succeeding. He concedes his great courage and strength to something outside of himself. The song reinforces the Church's message that without belief in something outside of ourselves, our souls will not be saved.

How to Accept That When it's Over, it's Over

Accounts of near-death experiences helped me cling to the afterlife myth for a long while. The anecdotal evidence from so many people had been enough proof for me until I saw well-documented research where the near-death experience is replicated in a lab. I had to rethink this last thread of "evidence." The scientific explanations not relying on the supernatural—the fading workings of a dying brain and seemingly real conversations with dead loved ones—were more convincing.

Since I now accept there is probably no afterlife, I look at life quite differently. First, because my focus is on life, second, because if this is all there is, I can revel in its true wonder more than I ever could before. Without fear there is freedom, and my life and the people in it have become even more precious.

> *The threat of external torment might scare some people into obedience, but it does nothing to inspire love. If you treated me with threats and intimidation, I would have to reconsider admiration of your character.*—Dan Barker, former minister turned atheist, author of *Godless*

In the 21st century, religion's hold on death continues to have some unfortunate consequences. If it wasn't for religion, I suspect that assisted dying would currently be allowed in Canada. It is the "compassion" of religion that allows our loved ones to suffer a lingering and excruciating death, leaving it in God's hands. With religion, people are not supposed to have control over their lives or over their deaths. I would prefer to decide, if the circumstance presents itself, to ensure an organized, legal, compassionate end to my suffering, rather than face an unnatural, medically extended, tormented life. My family would respect this and would welcome it, for my sake. This subject is complex enough without interference from religion. How can we offer more compassion and common sense to our beloved pets, whose inevitable deaths we facilitate with a veterinarian's gentle help? Of course, no one wishes to let loved ones go, but watching them suffer a long painful death, if their wish is to die on their own terms, contradicts love and compassion. I hope when my time comes and if it's due to a terminal illness, that there is a law in place similar to the one in the state of Oregon, USA, and in other countries, where people can freely and legally choose to end their life if they are terminally ill. For the sake of my loved ones, I want to be in a mental and physical state to have the opportunity to peacefully and painlessly say goodbye to them.

Unfortunately, tragedy or dying can also be used as an opportunity for the most vulnerable to convert. During this time of inquiry I was waiting to visit someone on the palliative floor of our local publicly funded hospital. I flipped open some small pastel-coloured pamphlets on display on a side table and started reading:

A Lost Soul on Judgment Morning

. . . A thousand tongues could ne'er describe
The anguish that I feel (Matthew 25:30,
Too late, too late now to repent,
Hell fire is all too REAL! (Mark 9:46)

Forever now while ages roll (Revelation 20:10),
My soul shall scream and burn,
Though torment reigns, my mind is clear (Luke 16:25)-
In life, God's love I spurned.
Forever doomed! . . .
. . . Dear friend, today a loving Lord
Would save you from this fate.
Come humbly now, accept His grace
Before it is too late!"[23]

*   *   *

At this time, I wanted to learn how secular people work through loss and grief without the perceived comfort of religion. I didn't have to look far to find groups who assist in a secular way. *Grief Beyond Belief* is one internet site that helps people to come to terms with death in a realistic and mature way. I have listened to several funeral sermons claiming that even if the deceased had not been overtly religious, their qualities had demonstrated that God was covertly working through them and so would surely take them home.

---

[23]   Gospel Tract & Bible Society Ste. Anne, Manitoba, Canada, Church of God in Christ, Mennonite

I hope that it will be said that I appreciated and celebrated this one precious life, that I embraced reason and compassion, and that I cared deeply about the people in my life. As it happens, I am not the only one who would prefer a secular ritual. When the topic has come up, some relatives and friends have expressed a similar desire. After a short time researching, I found that secular funerals are on the rise, in Canada and in other countries as well.[24]

Finding Peace

> *Live in optimism without the fear of judgment and death. There is enough purpose and meaning in life, love and leaving a good legacy. Oppose the danger of religious zealotry with the liberating belief that life on earth is precious because this here and now is all there is, and our destiny is in our own hands.*—Polly Toynbee, Journalist

When I decided to no longer be a part of the Catholic religion, I didn't call the Vatican or notify the local bishop, but I did understand that if there really was a heaven, I was now officially off the guest list. I could no longer choose to be a part of a misogynistic, oppressive, marginalizing organization built on fear and control. If I chose to remain silent, I would be supporting the travesty. My asking questions and speaking up is not about persecuting Catholics or other religious people. It is about no longer accepting the horrible treatment of others.

---

[24]   http://www.carnells.com/help-support-article.aspx?id=19

I feel embarrassed that I once believed that salvation could not come outside of the Catholic Church. When I see a crucifix, I no longer see a symbol of love and self-sacrifice; I see a story of a parent's human sacrifice of his son—such a drastic choice to forgive the sinful nature that he created in his children. The late comedian Lenny Bruce said, "If Jesus had been killed 20 years ago, Catholic school children would be wearing little electric chairs around their necks instead of crosses." Even a simple polite expression, "God bless you" following a sneeze seems strange and misplaced to me now—and just another way that God is infused into everyone's daily lives, whether we're religious or not.

I can't pretend to believe or have faith for my extended family's or community's sake. I will continue to seek out evidence for any claims made, regarding religion or any other idea. Other than the cover up of the rampant child rape, and the horrific stories of the treatment of Muslim women in the name of religion, I am less angry now that some of the shock has worn off. I learned more about religion and the history of the atrocities done in its name as I was leaving it, than I had learned in four decades practicing it. Maybe I only had the ability to think critically about it because I was on my way out. I have practiced my God-attributed free will to make the transition to a free and peaceful secular life. Once I applied critical thinking principals to religious concepts, I never did understand how our will could be free if, when we choose differently than God's will, he has an especially "warm" place for us after death. Ty's friend once told him that he feels sorry for atheists because they have nowhere to go after death. I had to chuckle. I wanted to say, "Actually, neither do you!" At least he was kind enough to say "nowhere"—rather than hell.

Accepting that there is no afterlife was the most liberating part of coming out. It was also the most difficult. I had believed in, and counted on the blissful idea of heaven for four decades. So, it makes sense that I will never begrudge the idea to others who choose to rely on it for comfort's sake. Whether I agree with them or not, I respect the freedom to believe different ideas, and I expect the same freedom.

*　　*　　*

I cherish my life more than I did as a believer as it is my one precious time to support and help others and to enjoy its beauty and wonder. For over a decade my career choice has been consistent with a philosophy of helping others. While setting aside religion and any sort of a biblical Higher Power in my personal life, I found it was a natural progression to experience a shift in thinking in my professional career. As I spent time thinking critically about the power of the supernatural, I naturally started to question the efficacy of an external locus of control in my professional field. My perception of a generic higher power had been forever altered by this new-found freedom from faith.

Chapter 10

Higher Power—and our Addictions

> *When we saw others solve their problems by a simple reliance upon the Spirit of the Universe, we had to stop doubting the power of God. Our ideas did not work. But the God idea did.*—Alcoholics Anonymous

I remember too well the day many years ago when I received a call about a relative who had been killed in a tragic accident. It was devastating news—the loss of a young life that was completely preventable. She was in her thirties and riding a bicycle on the highway for a fundraiser for her community when a drunk driver hit her. This horrible tragedy influenced my decision to apply for the director's position of a correctional facility for impaired drivers. I had already spent five years in the field of substance abuse working directly with offenders in a federal prison and later as a trainer of program officers for the prairie region.

The past nine and a half years have been spent in an administrative/program development capacity at the smaller correctional facility for impaired drivers. Despite a less hands-on role, my passion for working in this area has never wavered. I was grateful to be given the opportunity to be a part of something so vital in the province. My focus continues to be on programming that can play a critical role in reducing harmful and dangerous choices related to substance use.

The program for impaired drivers includes a primarily cognitive behavioural approach which assists clients in moving through stages of change. The objective is for the client to ultimately take responsibility for their choices and ideally to move forward without problematic drinking. The program also includes Twelve Step support such as Alcoholics Anonymous, Narcotics Anonymous and Al Anon. Volunteers come in from the community in the evenings with information about this type of support.

Throughout my involvement in the field, I always had to admire people who described how their lives were saved by involvement in such programs. Years ago I had a friend who drank too much; he never seemed to be able to drink without drinking in excess. Actually everything he did was extreme. Then, one day, he drove drunk and almost killed himself. Soon after, he joined a group and has lived crime-free and substance-free ever since. There is no denying the power of involvement in A.A. Admitting that one is powerless over an addiction and surrendering that power and will to a Higher Power is key. I always respected the fellowship of men and women who shared the desire to quit drinking and who supported each other unconditionally. From a Christian perspective—I was still a believer through most of this career—it wasn't a leap for me to accept that people were not alone in their desire to change their drinking habits, their environments, their entire lives; they had the assistance of power outside of themselves. I quietly hoped (and prayed) that everyone with substance abuse problems would attend A.A. and stay involved in the successful program. It seemed to me the best solution to a very complex and costly problem in our society.

Through my training and experience, I had become familiar with different theories of why people choose to abuse substances and was aware that not everyone responds to the same types of options for treatment or support. Even so, nothing in existence compared to the 24-hour support of Twelve Step fellowship. I saw the success of the program as evidence, albeit anecdotal, that God would help if he was sought out, as promised in the *Alcoholics Anonymous Big Book.* Small cards distributed at an informational meeting also put the focus on this Higher Power:

> Seven Truths that Bring Peace of Mind
> That things temporal are of little value.
> That the highest value should be put on things eternal.
> That there is absolutely no profit in sin.
> That we can never exceed God in generosity.
> That the pursuit of pleasure usually ends in pain.
> That God hates selfishness and loves generosity.
> That gratitude to God pays big dividends.

The faith-based aspect of the philosophy and the religiosity in the program is significant: there are 298 references to God in the *AA Big Book* and *The Twelve Steps and Twelve Traditions.*[25] Its context in the references is consistent with the personal God of the Bible. A.A. was developed, after all, by two Christian Caucasian males in a place and time when Christianity was considered sacrosanct.

---

[25] 164 and More. http://www.164andmore.com/words/god. htm, accessed April 14, 2012.

Early on in my career, I became curious when I found out approximately 5 to15 percent continued to attend A.A. meetings.[26] This percentage represents millions of people around the globe whose lives were saved through their involvement in the program. I discovered though, that many who chose not to attend or to stop attending were turned off by the faith-based part of the program. I started to wonder if the program could be more inclusive, regardless of belief system. As much as I admired the Twelve Step programs, it was evident that they weren't for everyone. Other options for support had to be available for people who chose not to attend.

If questioned about the religiosity of the program, many A.A. members explain that the "God" of the program doesn't have to be God but anything outside of oneself that the problem can be handed over to. Some call this just Good Orderly Direction. After all, they argue, it is their own arrogance that got them into trouble in the first place—thinking that they could handle addiction on their own, so it made sense to them that the solution would involve giving up control to an outside power. Incidentally, it is for this reason that some Christians criticize the program and claim that this more general interpretation of "God" is blasphemous.

The Language

> *. . . usually, men and women who are constitutionally incapable of being honest with*

---

[26] Nancy Snyderman 20/20 ABC News 2001 "Are You in Control?"

> *themselves. There are such unfortunates. They*
> *are not at fault; they seem to be born that way.*
> *They are naturally incapable of grasping and*
> *developing a manner of living which demands*
> *rigorous honesty. Their chances are less than*
> *average. There are those, too, who suffer grave*
> *emotional disorders, but many of them do*
> *recover if they have the capacity to be honest.*
> (A.A.)

I was listening to a program on the local radio station one day when the guest was speaking about a youth treatment centre in another province and describing its philosophy. He explained how the youth ask for help from someone [God] who knows more than them, and that it's spirituality not religiosity. He said that the program was faith-based, and that the youth are told that they have a horrific disease, a mental illness, and a brain disease, and that they have a chronic terminal illness.

This seemed less than supportive. When I called the centre years ago for more information on treatment centres for youth, the person answering the phone described the program as faith-based and developed around the philosophy of Twelve Step programs. The woman explained that the youth were required to participate in the Twelve Steps and that they were provided a timeframe in which to progress through them; if they failed, they were required to leave the facility. It was a condition that they internalized one particular model of treatment. I sat back in my chair with a disheartened sigh.

Even as a person of faith at that time, this phone conversation increased my determination to help provide inclusive options for support to people, no matter their age or belief system. I have witnessed how people can change without belief in a Higher Power when they quit smoking, or change their eating or drinking habits. Whatever the belief or support system, the individual must take responsibility and make the necessary changes.

When I looked more closely at the *Alcoholics Anonymous Big Book*, I was a little disheartened to see the language used: "flaws in our makeup," "defects of character," "mentally and physically ill," "spiritually sick," and "constitutionally incapable of being honest."[27] I could see how some might see the language as limiting or marginalizing, and would prefer the language of empowerment rather than powerlessness and disease. Some might prefer to be told that they could make different choices and that they are solely responsible for changing behaviour. Some might want to know that no matter their religious or spiritual belief, that they are constitutionally capable of being honest and taking full responsibility for their choices.

If I was told that I was one of the "unfortunates" born somehow incapable of changing my lifestyle, I would feel hopeless. The reality is, no matter the constitution, people usually change when the pain of not changing becomes greater than making the changes.

Fortunately, the program works for people who choose it, however only a small percentage of people needing help choose it. The language may have been more acceptable in the past, but to many it may be too similar to the deprecatory language of another popular book, the Bible. The writers, the founders of A.A. had of course based their religiosity in the Big Book on the Judeo-Christian holy book.

---

[27]   *Alcoholics Anonymous* Fourth Edition, Alcoholics Anonymous World Services Inc., New York City, 2001. 58

Michele Ketzmerick

For The Atheists and Agnostics

> *As soon as we admitted the possible existence of a Creative Intelligence, a Spirit of the Universe underlying the totality of things, we began to be possessed of a new sense of power and direction, provided we took other simple steps. We found God does not make too hard terms with those who seek Him* (A.A.)

One chapter of *Alcoholics Anonymous* is called "We Agnostics." When I first read it as a Catholic, I was intrigued to see a chapter meant specifically for nonbelievers. Later, when I started having doubts about my religion, I appreciated the idea of spirituality versus religion. Explanations from people involved with the program satisfied my believing nature at that time.

Rereading the book after years of working in the field and now from a sceptic's perspective, I discovered that the chapter for atheists and agnostics is not about including those who do not believe in God, but rather about how nonbelievers can become believers. The chapter is about the conversion experience and what it means to believe in a Higher Power. The examples describe people who started as agnostics or nonbelievers and who were eventually able to accomplish the goal of turning their lives over to God. It's one thing to say that's not what is really meant, but there is no denying the religiosity throughout the *Big Book*, and in the prayers recited at every meeting.

I could now understand why some people, who desperately needed help but who were turned off by this perceived religiosity, felt excluded based on their beliefs. It does sound more inclusive when the program is referred to

122

as *spiritual not religious*, but secular people would remain excluded with the claim of an invisible power outside of us.

> *Without help it is too much for us. But there is One who has all power—that One is God. May you find Him now!* (A.A.)

Are They Just Selfish?

> *Above everything, we alcoholics must be rid of this selfishness. We must, or it kills us! God makes that possible. And there often seems no way of entirely getting rid of self without His aid. Many of us had moral and philosophical convictions galore, but we could not live up to them even though we would have liked to. Neither could we reduce our self-centeredness much by wishing or trying on our own power. We had to have God's help.* (A.A.)

How many people were taught at a young age how capable they were, and how to take care of themselves in a healthy way? I have learnt the hard way that if I do not take care of myself, I will not be able to take care of others properly. During the time of the debilitating pain in my back, I was forced to evaluate my hectic lifestyle and career, and to consciously take time to pause. This philosophy is about taking responsibility rather than about being selfish.

If we do not deal with stress or emotional pain in our lives—because we are so busy taking care of everyone else—we may eat or drink too much, use over-the-counter or illicit drugs, or gamble in excess. The result means neglecting our loved ones, our jobs, ourselves. Then we blame selfishness as the culprit for unhealthy coping strategies.

Behind stories of substance abuse are stories of pain, neglect, and lack of coping skills. There is also a lack of belief and confidence that a person can change, or has the power or ability to do so. I wondered if it was still necessary to break down people's self confidence, when abuse and neglect were part of the original problem. Many people who choose to abuse substances are already broken down and this is one form of coping. They do not feel that they deserve a better life, and more importantly, that they personally can make it happen.

Although often complex and difficult to deal with, there is little mystery to addiction. There isn't a blood test that can be administered to children to show that some are doomed to an eventual life of substance abuse. It isn't that alcohol is cunning or baffling—it is an addictive substance. Any human being who uses an excessive amount of alcohol over a long period of time will experience physical and psychological problems associated with the use. Nicotine is also an addictive substance that, no matter who chooses to inhale it, the body and mind will crave it when discontinued.

The Best Placebo Effect in History

The Wikipedia definition of cognitive dissonance is "the discomfort caused by holding conflicting ideas simultaneously." I went for a walk one day during my lunch break. As I breathed in the fresh air, I thought about the huge change that I had experienced in letting go of my belief in God and religion, and how that had changed my perspective on so many things. I valued my life and relationships in a more significant and profound way; I viewed mistakes and poor choices differently; and of course I had lost the exaggerated fear of death and the afterlife. I returned to my office and suddenly realized that this insight could shift my thinking about substance abuse as well.

What would happen if I applied the same principles of critical thinking to the Higher Power idea in substance abuse treatment? Until then I had just accepted that the belief in the assistance of a power outside of themselves seemed to work for some. But discounting the existence of a Higher Power, who or what is really "fixing" people? What if the magic is really in the strength of the individual and the power of the unwavering support and kindness of others?

My admiration for people who make difficult changes in their lives with the support they find in Twelve Step programs has never changed, even as my belief in all things supernatural has. Actually, my admiration for them has grown. What I realize now is that the concept of a Higher Power is probably the most magnificent placebo. Who is really dong the fixing? Does it matter that there really isn't an outside force assisting, or that success might be due to the social and psychological aspects and support of the dedicated people in the program? A critical part of success—no matter what type of treatment modality—is spending time with supportive people who choose not to drink or use drugs. Success is due to the commitment of the individual, rather than the power of the spirit. Rather than consider power flowing in from an outside source that we must be worthy of receiving, it might be helpful to acknowledge more fully, the power inside of us, our personal strength. Taking responsibility and changing one's life is the opposite of selfishness or arrogance.

A New Way

It can be challenging to discuss different ways of thinking about substance abuse treatment when the industry has long been associated with only one type of support. There is no denying the degree of efficacy with a one-size-fits-all approach, a faith-based model, such as Twelve Steps, but it is evident by the lack of attendance, or continued attendance, that this approach is not for everyone. With my new insights, I wondered how some of the underlying principles of A.A. could be tweaked and updated to reflect a philosophy where this same type of support could be offered without the parts that turn people away—such as the disparaging language leftover from an earlier era. The language of empowerment, personal strength, responsibility, and choice sounded more conducive to promoting change.

The most difficult addiction to quit is nicotine and most people who quit, do so on their own without ever acknowledging a Higher Power. They choose to continue to smoke, not because they are born with a disease or because they are selfish or incapable of being honest, but because the substance is addictive. It doesn't matter who it is, or who his or her parents or grandparents are, if an addictive substance is regularly ingested, injected, or inhaled, many people will continue use despite physical, psychological, or social problems. Also, cessation of the substance will result in the unpleasant experience of withdrawal. People continue despite the dangers, usually because the physical and psychological effects of withdrawal are too unpleasant, and their environments are not conducive to supporting or maintaining the change. Smokers might choose not to change, or they might decide to empower themselves to choose otherwise. The threat of cancer may outweigh the discomfort of quitting, for instance.

If the Twelve Step approach was not faith-based it would logically be more inclusive but until that happens, other options are necessary. One such option is for those who would prefer meetings without prayers or religiosity is called Secular Organization for Sobriety. It is a worldwide organization with the first group in our province established in 2011. SOS is a non-faith-based support group with the emphasis on taking responsibility for choices related to substance use. Without diminishing the efficacy of Twelve Step programs, it offers an option for support for those who choose not to attend Twelve Step programs.

If the *Big Book* was updated to speak to all people—believers or not—I suspect that it would not disrespect the great accomplishment of the Christian founders, or of the millions of men and women in the program since that time. The world is a very different place than when A.A. was developed in the 1930s. I understood that the gentle suggestion to update the Big Book or to make it more relevant in the 21st Century would be coming from an unlikely source, but few people in the program would argue against making it even more inclusive. I also understood that the likelihood of that happening would be similar to updating the Bible.

No matter what their belief, everyone can be helped by A.A. because it is made up of millions of supportive people. With more inclusive language, without prayers at meetings or a "God" philosophy woven through, even more people might be helped. That is one truly great message of hope that has come out of my inquiry.

I propose a secular recovery testimonial:

> **All this time I thought that it was actually something outside of me fixing my problems when it's been me all along! I'm not "less than" other human beings and I'm not doomed because of my DNA; I am constitutionally capable of being honest; I can fix what I messed up; I don't believe in the supernatural or something outside of me taking over; I am not spiritually, mentally or physically ill; I am responsible and can manage my life—and although unaware of this, I have been managing my life well, believing that it was something or someone else doing the heavy lifting. I don't have an incurable disease for life—I was drinking to cope with other things, complex things, challenging things, and although extremely difficult, I made the necessary changes in my life. I am capable of succeeding. I have the strength to succeed. The group is what helped me to succeed. I did it with their support, their company and an environment that does not involve drinking.**

Earlier, after critiquing the Ten Commandments, I shared my idea for a revised 21st century version. I hereby also offer a Secular Ten Steps to recovery, developed as a revision of the Twelve Steps. (There are two fewer steps because the original has God/spirituality/prayer infused throughout seven of the steps):

A Secular Ten Steps:

1. Admitted that we had made negative choices regarding substance use and that our lives had become unmanageable as a result.
2. Came to believe that we were responsible for our choices and that we had the strength and power to change our lives.
3. Made a decision to take full responsibility to do what is necessary to make positive choices in all areas of our lives.
4. Made a searching inventory of our past choices.
5. Admitted to ourselves and to another human being the exact nature of our negative choices.
6. Were entirely ready to make a commitment to change.
7. Made a list of everyone affected by our negative choices.
8. Apologized to those that were affected as a result of our choices, except when to do so would further harm others.
9. Continued to work at making positive choices in all areas of life.
10. Having made significant changes in our lives with the support of a compassionate community of people with similar challenges, we committed to helping others to realize their personal strength and potential in doing the same.

Chapter 11

Coming Out and Moving Forward

> *We can and should critique religion just as much as we can and critically think about any ideas, opinions and philosophies. If faith will not bear to be investigated; if its preachers and professors are afraid to have it examined, their foundation must be very weak.*—George A. Smith, early leader in The Church of Jesus Christ of Latter-day Saints

When I was one of the faithful I believed that it was wrong to question religion. I regret now that I waited so long to find the courage to do so. It was just easier—and more comfortable not to. In every other area of my life, I asked for evidence, I *googled*, I checked out at least three other sources for every claim. Finally, I had to include religion in my list of ideas subject to critical thinking because beliefs, after all, are just ideas.

I realized that just because many people believe something doesn't make it so. The illiterate masses believed in bloodletting, in numerous gods, and that natural disasters were punishment from God. God used to be everything when people knew less. Fortunately, he has become the answer for less as science provides more facts about earthquakes, the solar system, and the shape and age of the earth (fundamentalist Christians still believe that the earth is only 6,000 years old). The floods and failed crops can no longer be considered the fault of witches, and earthquakes and tsunamis the fault of homosexuals because we know more about natural disasters, germs and causes of disease, and we no longer spit in wounds or condemn small pox vaccination as violating God's will. In enlightened countries, science continues to narrow the gap of knowledge that once defaulted to God.

During the researching and writing, as I discreetly let go of being Catholic, I chose to do so without sharing my change of heart with any close theists in my life. This still seemed too risky somehow. I found that I was able to talk about it as long as the people in the discussion weren't close to me. When I asked acquaintances about their religious beliefs and they'd say they were "Catholic but not practicing anymore," I wondered, could they be truly Catholic then? Did they know what being Catholic really meant? The other response I heard was, "I'm spiritual, not religious." This was usually from people who had already realized the divisiveness and fallacy of religion but—despite lack of evidence, and probably due to the comfort factor—were not yet ready to leave the supernatural or superstitions behind.

I understood the reluctance to come out as a nonbeliever, the feeling of dread and not wanting to be ostracized especially within a religious culture, for believing differently. But, I now feel that as difficult as it is, hiding my true self is not an honest way to live. My theist friends and relatives do not deserve that from me. When I choose to share this journey of inquiry with them, my sincere hope is that they quickly realize that I am still the person that they have shared their love with.

In my religious past, atheist for me meant evil Satan-worshipper and it was difficult to rid myself of the preconceived idea. It took almost two decades to realize the man sleeping next to me was one of them! Now atheism to me just means absence of belief in any gods. The concept has changed from a scary manipulation imposed by religion to something benign. The non-believers in my life—at least the ones of whom I am aware—are peaceful, kind, generous people.

"Isn't atheism just another religion?" I was asked by one of my brothers. "Atheism is a religion like 'off' is a TV channel." (Monicks.net, atheist blog) Atheism is just absent of any religion so how could it be a religion? It lacks any type of dogma, rules, rituals, or a belief in god(s) or the supernatural. It is absent of the manipulative concept of sin, divine judgment, or anointed privileged groups such as holy leaders. It has no holy book, miracles, afterlife, creeds or origin myths. Nonbelievers don't use fear or push for obedience. A key difference between the faithful and nonbelievers is that a non-believer would change his or her thinking about the supernatural if it was proved otherwise by science. Scientific reasoning is absent in religion—it is discouraged because it indicates a lack of faith. Applying scientific reasoning to religion would most likely result in a crisis of faith as it did for me. Hopefully, eventually, more theists will feel comfortable questioning why they claim to know something that they really don't. People can rely on their internal compasses, their inner strength, and each other, rather than an external power that doesn't exist.

As Sam Harris explains very simply, "No one ever needs to identify himself as a 'non-astrologer' or a 'non-alchemist.'

We do not have words for people who doubt that Elvis is still alive or that aliens have traversed the galaxy only to molest ranchers and their cattle. Atheism is nothing more than the noises reasonable people make in the presence of unjustified religious beliefs."[28]

Even as I was nearing the end of writing, I found it difficult to call myself atheist. I can't say with certainty that some impersonal universal force doesn't exist, but I have yet to hear a convincing argument that God does. The Bible convinced me that the existence of a personal deity is most unlikely. With anything less than 100% certainty, this would be considered agnosticism. These are some basic definitions that helped me to understand commonly used terms around belief:

- Theism—Belief in a personal god (or gods).
- Atheism—Absence of belief in any god.
- Agnosticism—Refusal to accept the truth of a proposition for which there is insufficient evidence or logical justification. Most agnostics suspend belief in a god.
- Freethought—The practice of forming opinions about religion based on reason, without reference to authority tradition or established belief.
- Humanism—Secular humanism is a rationalistic, natural outlook that makes humanity the measure of values.[29]

---

[28] Sam Harris *Letter to a Christian Nation*. (Random House, Vintage Books, 2008), 51

[29] Dan Barker, *Godless* (Berkeley, CA: Ulysses Press, 2008), 118-119

If I must be labelled, I prefer "sceptic" (one who doubts the truth of a religious belief, according to the dictionary), or just a non-religious person. Since I began sharing my scepticism with people, I have learned that there are others who've had the same thoughts, and who are equally relieved to hear that their questions and feelings are not only shared, but valid. These are people who could not resolve the cognitive dissonance and who eventually arrived at the same place as I. Their research processes had similar conclusions to mine: simply, Adam and Eve could not have existed; every religion couldn't be right; and evolution is a scientifically proven fact. As Carl Sagan said, "Extraordinary claims require extraordinary evidence." I had been taught a lot of things based on wishful thinking, comfort, and speculation. I eventually could not see having faith as a virtue, or the point in rewarding blind faith. I had once believed in hell because it was a sin not to, and then stopped believing in hell because there was absolutely no evidence to support its existence. Disbelief in the rest soon followed.

Once I learned more I couldn't go back. I couldn't pretend. Because of this process of inquiry, I understood now how it was better for religion if we did not investigate, if we did not critically think about why we believed the things that we did.

Coming Out . . . Slowly

> *For me, it is far better to grasp the universe as it really is, than to persist in delusion however satisfying and reassuring.*—Carl Sagan

By this time in my conversion, I had also let go of the generic spirituality (and anything else esoteric or not of our natural world), and was ready to talk about religion or spirituality with people closer to me. It wasn't long afterwards that I had a discussion with a relative. I was so relieved to find out that she felt the same way and we were so excited to share our thoughts, it was comical: both of us talking quickly and loudly, and mostly at the same time. It was so good to be understood and accepted as a non-religious person. I felt less alone moving forward. We have kept in closer touch ever since, sharing great books and stories.

On three other occasions though, when the topic of religion surfaced, I shared some of the things that I had learned, to the surprise and amusement of people. The first occasion was during a Christmas party for Ty's hockey team. One of the parents asked why Ty had moved from a Catholic school to a public school. I told the stories about the harmful messages that were being taught regarding sexual health and Catholic dogma and the discussion continued for a few hours. We talked about older religions, and about some of the strange origins and beliefs in Mormonism and Scientology. I was trying to be cautious and respectful of the people in the room, so as not to offend any strong theists or Scientologists. The questions from the group were similar to the ones that prompted this process of inquiry for me. How can people claim to know that God really exists? What really happens when we die? What about just having faith? What about being spiritual not religious? We talked about the peculiarity of newer belief systems like Jehovah's Witness, Scientology, and Mormonism, but came to the same conclusion that they are no more bizarre than Catholics consuming the actual body and drinking the actual blood of Jesus in the magic of the mass. The group of parents was shocked to learn about the extent of the priestly pedophilia and further disgusted at the systematic, decades-long cover up. Though a rather strange discussion for a Christmas party, it felt liberating to finally talk with people I knew, about the religious things that I had mostly kept to myself. I was not trying to be the authority on the subject, rather just participating in a discussion, and sharing common questions and doubts about belief systems.

Although my relationships with the hockey parents seemed the same for the remainder of the season, there were times I noticed a subtle change with one parent in particular. Maybe I was just overly sensitive when residual Catholic guilt surfaced for daring to speak up.

The second instance was during the Christmas holidays, while visiting with long time friends, as well as all of their family. The group consisted of some baptized, some not baptized, some no longer religious, some Protestants, and my Catholic brother and sister-in-law. Somehow the topic of religion came up and I shared that I was in the middle of writing a book about religion, more specifically my journey out of it. My heart was beating faster than usual because this was the first time that any of my siblings would know what I was up to. The Protestants shared their views of some of the Catholics that they knew who claim to be very devout on Sundays but are rude and unkind the rest of the week, and the non-religious voiced with certainty that people can be good without religion. Similar questions as the ones at the hockey party flew around the room, including whose religion is the right one and what about psychics and New Age beliefs? I smiled when someone mentioned that Hitler was Catholic. Theists often use the Nazi leader as an example of how atheists inflict suffering and death on the world. I had once thought that atheists were responsible for the atrocities in the world such as wars and genocide until I realized (early in this time of questioning my faith) that fascist leaders and the cult of religious hero worship were more to blame. I hadn't known that written in German on the belt buckles of Hitler's soldiers was "God on our side," in German, and that his Catholic religiosity was clearly evident in his speeches and book, *Mein Kampf.* [30]

As I expanded on the reasons for leaving faith, the discussion unexpectedly turned very serious and heart wrenching. This family had lost a loved one very suddenly just eighteen months earlier. They were dealing with the sort of grief and loss that I had never experienced. Some expressed anger that God could allow something so unthinkable. There was some discussion about hanging on to the hope that whether we have evidence for it or not, there must be something more. Understandably, the more sceptical of the group wanted assurance that we would be reunited with loved ones again. The pain of anything less would be too much for this family, and although I wanted to have the answers for their questions about death and the afterlife, I was not capable of providing any honest comfort. I also wanted to reinforce that whatever belief they find comfort in was not right or wrong—that we just do what's necessary in devastating circumstances.

It was getting late and the discussion became more emotional. There was anger and heavy sadness. What started out as me joking about my book on religion had turned into a dynamic discussion and left sobering questions

---

[30] Hitler's Religious Beliefs and Fanaticism. (Selected quotes from Mein Kampf), compiled by Jim Walker, originated: 28 Nov. 1996, accessed on April 22, 2012. http://nobeliefs.com/hitler.htm.

hanging in air. I felt remorse the following morning and had a short discussion with my brother and his wife. I also felt exposed and vulnerable to criticism because I disclosed this significant shift of thinking to the first of several theistic family members. I wanted reassurance that I wouldn't be regarded differently or judged by them. More importantly I didn't want to offend this grieving family.

It was an experience that caused me to suspend the writing process for several weeks. During that time I contemplated the comfort part of the God story—the part where people find necessary solace in times of unimaginable grief. True or not, this hope to be reunited in an afterlife is difficult to let go, regardless of the acknowledgment that this same God that promises solace was impotent in stopping the tragedy in the first place. During the weeks following, it became vividly clear why religion was developed by humanity and how its continuity is solidly supported by the human need to soften the potent sting of death.

Even if I know that it's not logical or rational, I suspect that I would, if faced with similar tragedy, want to believe that something exists beyond this life, that death is not the end. It might be easier to accept an afterlife that we have no evidence for, than to accept that tragedy and illness, unfortunately, just happens. Although I doubt that I will return to faith, when tragedy and loss occur in my life, I would most likely now skip the "crisis of faith" stage and move on to the inevitable and difficult process of grieving.

> ***Death belongs to life itself. There is nothing but this world, this life, the present. The world is beautiful and outside there is no salvation . . . Death is bitter and absurd. In accepting this, one most intensely appreciates what we have***

and know.—Ronald Aronson, author of *Living Without God: New Directions for Atheists, Agnostics, Secularists, and the Undecided*

The third occasion of speaking with others about religion was on a sunny summer afternoon, socializing with friends at a nearby lake. I was telling them about an interesting book that I was reading called *The Psychopath Test* by Jon Ronson. I had ordered the book after I saw the author on one of the late-night talk shows. I was telling them about how a Scientologist had been involved in the story and realized that I was mocking the absurdity of Scientology as I was telling the story. I stopped myself, quickly apologized, and asked if the man or his wife were Scientologists. They started laughing and said that they weren't religious people. As the discussion progressed I was so excited to learn that we had similar favourite secular authors, and then had to laugh as we automatically lowered our voices as if discussing something forbidden. They, too, were sceptical of religion and the supernatural, and it was like finding long lost kin. We spoke quickly and quietly and were giddy to have the freedom to express our real thoughts about religion. Suddenly, out of respect for the theists joining us, the topic changed.

Moving Forward

Isn't it enough to see that a garden is beautiful without having to believe that there are fairies at the bottom of it too?—Douglas Adams, English humorist & science fiction novelist

139

There was no dramatic announcement that I left Catholicism. I didn't arrange meetings to share that I no longer held any belief in a deity, and I haven't made a point of telling religious family members that I no longer believe in God. It may seem like cowardice and I admit to some of that, but I needed to sort through so much to eventually understand the conversion myself. I didn't have the energy or desire to be challenged during the process. I was purposely discreet and secretive, and usually fragile and somewhat nervous.

When I chose to share with others, I enjoyed the experience, especially with those who want so much to believe for the comfort of it, but know in their heart of hearts that much of it makes little sense. I have also met people who admit that they don't really know why they believe as they do, that their beliefs, like mine, had been handed down by their parents, through church attendance and faith-based schools. For some, whether it's true or not does not matter. They will choose to go through life not wanting to question, in the hopes that there is heaven after death where we will all meet again. Sam Harris, author of *The End of Faith* describes this unfortunate but common phenomenon as having "an insufficient taste for evidence." I understand the power of this kind of belief, but what is true and what is comforting are two different things.

The fear that life would be meaningless without religion kept me faithful, even though all along it was not religion that was making my life meaningful—it was the people in my life. Now, more than ever I treasure this life. I continue to experience peace, love, wonder and awe and none of these come from religion.

I also continued to notice things that I never would have been sensitive to as a believer. As I sat down to enjoy Kara's university convocation, the ceremony began with a prayer. I would not have thought twice about this imposition a few years ago. The ceremony ended with a loud live band playing "God Save the Queen." Was it presumed that everyone believes in God and prays? This was an institution of science, of academia. It was insensitive, and an imposition, I felt, to infuse religion and God into a non-religious ceremony.

I became angry also when I learned of the proselytizing that accompanies the good missionary work in the Church, along with the deadly message regarding condom use passed down from an irresponsible head of the Catholic Church.

I married a person who belongs to the segment of society that I was taught by religion to fear and to blame for all the evil in the world. From my underlying arrogance and judgment of praying for his conversion, to learning about morality from my non-religious husband, this transformation has made me humble. I first saw Murray as unfortunate for not learning the truth at a young age and lacking the foundation of faith, and now I regard him as fortunate to have grown up without indoctrination. I envy the fact that he is loved by religious relatives for the good person that he is, and regret that I may be regarded differently for finding my way to his same place. I may be judged for coming out, but he will not be judged for never being in. I am grateful that our values overshadowed my liberal religious beliefs as we parented our three kids together.

Finally, I appreciate more than ever that I married a nonbeliever, a person who is absent any religious belief or belief in god(s), an atheist. Although he lacks any experiential understanding of the struggle out of cultural religious conditioning, we find the common ground of reason is a great place to be. I also appreciate the freedom that I have to write about religion. It wasn't long ago in our history that I would have been burned at the stake as commanded by the God in the Bible. It saddens me greatly that this *heresy* is still forbidden and punishable by death in other religions. I appreciate where I live because unlike women in other countries, I do not fear being stoned, beheaded or shunned in the name of religion.

When I asked a religious relative to explain how an atheist could be so loving, generous, and kind, he explained that whether Murray believed in God or not, that it was God working inside of him, that his goodness is proof of God working in his life. How theists can give a non-existent entity the credit for someone's integrity and moral character remains a problem for me.

Despite the infusion of religion that continues today in our country, I am excited about the serious discussion surrounding end-of-life decision-making in Canada, and I am confident that soon compassion will prevail. I am also pleased to hear about a supportive organization called The Clergy Project for former and existing clergy who can no longer believe in the supernatural. In the pulpit or not, they are now secular humanists, freethinkers, atheists, or other types of non-theists.[31]

Religious beliefs should be subjected to the same kinds of conversational pressure as all other beliefs do. It is taboo that religion gets a free

---

[31] Hemant Mehta, "The Clergy Project: A Sanctuary for Religious Refugees," accessed April 22, 2012. http://www.patheos. com/blogs/friendlyatheist/2011/10/09/the-clergy-project-a-sanctuary-for-religious-refugees/

***ride—this has to change. It's okay to have a
discussion about it.***—Sam Harris

*   *   *

It is difficult to sum up my transition because change will
never stop occurring and because I will never stop the
exciting adventure of learning and challenging my own
thinking and belief system. I am content in this place of
reason.

More than anything, I am pleased that many people
are speaking out about the imposition of religion in our
everyday lives: about everything from stem cell research,
birth control and sexual health, dying with dignity, to
prayer at public events and our national anthem. My ideas
and opinions are just that, and will undoubtedly differ
from others'. I did not come to these conclusions lightly
and did not take anything on faith. I took the search for
answers very seriously and I am completely satisfied to no
longer believe that we are born broken, sinners by default,
trying to follow rules that are ever changing. Maybe there is
something more, something different to the claims made by
the world religions. I would be relieved to learn about some
cosmic meeting ground for all our units of energy to gather
and celebrate after we die. As a theist I was quite certain of
God and my faith, and was reluctant to look outside of it.
The tenets of my religion were absolutes but my non-belief
would change if evidence presented itself.

Although I have failed to find some reliable evidence
for the supernatural, other realms of existence, the soul, or
other lives, a part of my brain holds out for it. I accept that
this is it, though, as far as I know now. I felt a sense of loss,
but also relief, to know that there is no heaven or hell. I

have admired, and am very grateful to, the many former believers whose stories I have immersed myself in, who have been courageous enough to come out. I encourage others to feel good about questioning beliefs of a lifetime and to critically think about the important topic of religion. It is okay to not believe in the status quo but to believe in ourselves, in kindness, in love, in respecting others, and in living a cherished life—because it is probably the only one we have.

Books and Websites Cited
or Recommended

Adams, Douglas. Quote found on http://www.quotations page.com/quotes/Douglas_Adams, and http://www.ncl. ac.uk/philosophical/the-project/book/2011/Betts.pdf

Alcoholics Anonymous World Services, *Alcoholics Anonymous.* Fourth Edition, 2001.

Anderson, Joan. *A Weekend to Change Your Life.* New York: Broadway Books, 2006.

Aronson, Ronald. *Living Without God.* California, Counterpoint, 2008.

Asimov, Isaac quotes found on http://richarddawkins.net/ quotes and http://www.chrisbeach.co.uk/viewQuotes. php?QuotePage=5

Aurelius, Marcus quote found on http://richarddawkins.net/ quotes and http://www.goodreads.com/quotes/show/ 63966

Ayaan Hirsi Ali. *Infidel.* New York: Free Press., 2007.

Ayaan Hirsi Ali. *Nomad.* Canada: Knopf Canada, 2010.

Barker, Dan. *Godless.* California: Ulysses Press, 2008.

Bible. *The Catholic Youth Bible.* All bible quotes were cross referenced with this New Revised Standard Version.

Blackford, Russell & Schuklenk, Udo (Edited by). *50 Voices of Disbelief: Why We Are Atheists.* Great Britain: Blackwell Publishing, Ltd., 2009.

Brayshaw, *Satan: Christianity's Other God*

Bruce, Lenny. Quote found on http://www.brainyquote. com/quotes/authors/l/lenny_bruce.html

Browne, Sylvia. *The Mystical Life of Jesus: An Uncommon Perspective on the Life of Christ.* New York: New American Library, 2006.

Catholic Church Sex Abuse Scandals Around the World in the website BBC News Europe. http://www.bbc.co.uk/ news/10407559

Chopra, Deepak. *Life After Death: The Burden of Proof.* New York: Three Rivers Press, 2006.

Darrow, Clarence quoted in *Evil Summer: Babe Leopold, Dickie Loeb, and the Kidnap-Murder of Bobby Franks,* by John Theodore, 2007.

Daleiden, Joseph. Quote found on http://calgaryhumanist. ca/ericsquotes.html and de Beauvoir, Simone. *The Second Sex,* 1949 quoted in the article Islam and Women's Rights on the website http://www.atheistfoundation. org.au/articles/islam-and-womens—rights

Dennett, Daniel C. *Breaking the Spell: Religion as a Natural Phenomenon.* London: Viking, 2006.

Dawkins, Richard. *The God Delusion.* New York: First Mariner Books, 2006.

Elder, Paul. *Eyes of an Angel: A true Story. Soul Travel, Spirit Guides, Soul Mates, and the Reality of Love.* Virginia: Hampton Roads Publishing Company Inc., 2005.

Haldane, J.B.S. Quote found on http://www. humanismbyjoe.com/religion_quotes.htm

Harpur, Tom. *The Pagan Christ: Recovering the Lost Light.* Toronto: Thomas Allen Publishers, 2004.

Harris, Sam. *Letter to a Christian Nation.* New York: Vintage Books, 2006, 2008.

Harris, Sam. *The End of Faith: Religion, Terror, and the Future of Reason.* New York, W.W.Norton & Company, Inc., 2004.

Hawking, Stephen. Quote found on http://www.oxelon.com/n/2011/05/16/stephen_hawking.html

Hitchens, Christopher. *God is Not Great: How Religion Poisons Everything.* Toronto: Emblem, 2007.

Hitchens, Christopher. *The Missionary Position: Mother Teresa in Theory and Practice.* London, New York: Verso, 1995.

Hitchens, Christopher. *The Portable Atheist: Essential Readings for the Nonbeliever,* Philadelphia, 2007.

Hughes, Rupert. Quote found on http://64.132.170.146/religion_quotes.htm and http://www.humanismbyjoe.co/religion-quotes/

Intelligence Squared Debate: Christopher Hitchens and Stephen Fry, 2009.

Jefferson, Thomas quotes found in http://www.nobeliefs.com/jefferson.htm and—Thomas Jefferson, letter to Peter Carr, August 10, 1787 and http://thinkexist.com/quotation/question_with_boldness_even_the_existence_of_god/190 463.html

Mencken, H.L. Quote found in http://quotationsbook.com/quote/11363/ and http://www.biology.ed.ac.uk/research/groups/tlittle/page1/page15/page15.html

Norton, Joan. *The Mary Magdalene Within.* Lincoln, NE USA: iUniverse, 2005.

Robertson, Jeoffrey. *The Case of the Pope: Vatican Accountability for Human Rights Abuse.* London: Penguin Books, 2010.

Russell, Bertrand. *Why I Am Not a Christian: and other essays on religion and related subjects.* New York: Touchstone, 1957.

Sample, Ian. Stephen Hawking: 'There is no heaven; it's a fairy story' http://www.guardian.co.uk/science/2011/may/15/stephen-hawking-interview-there-is-no-heaven

Shermer, Michael. *The Believing Brain: From Ghosts and Gods to Politics and Conspiracies—How We Construct Beliefs and Reinforce Them as Truths.* New York: Times Books, 2011.

Smith, George A. 1871, Journal of Discourses, Vol 14, p 216 on website called "Mormons in Transition," Authority Claims of LDS Leaders, accessed May 2, 2012. http://www.irr.org/mit/wdist/authority-claims.html

Stanton, Elizabeth Cady. Quoted in the website The Dark Bible, Women's Inferior Status, accessed April 26, 2012. http://www.nobeliefs.com/DarkBible/darkbible7.htm

Steinbeck, John. http://www.goodreads.com/quotes/show/68226 and http://thinkexist.com/quotes/john_steinbeck/

Sweeney, Julia. *Letting go of God.* Found on http://www.youtube.com/watch?v=Bqh53RCkURQ, accessed June 25, 2012

Thomson, Anderson Jr. with Clare Aukofer. *Why We Believe in God(s).* Virginia: Pitchstone Publishing, 2011.

Twain, Mark quote found on http://richarddawkins.net/quotes?utf8=%E2%9C%93&search%5Bauthor_eq%5D=Mark+ Twain and http://www.twainquotes.com/Religion.html

Walsch, Neale Donald. *Conversations with God.* Books 1, 2, 3 Hampton Roads Publishing Co. 1995, 2002, 2003,

Weinberg, Steven. Quote found on http://relijournal. com/religion/top-ten-quotes-against-religion/   and http://www.goodreads.com/author/quotes/86758. Steven_Weinberg

Weiss, Brian. *Many Lives, Many Masters.* New York: Fireside, 1998.

Young, Paul. *The Shack.* California: Windblown Media, 2007.

http://mirandaceleste.net/tag/catholicism/

http://www.humanismbyjoe.com/religion_quotes.htm

http://www.postmormon.org/exp_e/index.php/ discussions/ . . . htm/ . . . /9389/

http://thinkexist.com/quotation

http://monicks.net/20

http://godisimaginary.com/i3.htm 11/01/15/my-quote-of-the-day/

http://www.commonwealmagazine.org/blog/?p=17960

Author Bio

Michele Ketzmerick earned a bachelor's degree in Human Justice, and teaches classes in the Correctional Studies Program at the Saskatchewan Institute of Applied Science and Technology. She lives outside a Saskatchewan city with her husband Murray; they have three children. Michele works as the Director of a correctional facility and treatment centre.

Dani Van Steelandt, Van Steelandt Photography

CPSIA information can be obtained at www.ICGtesting.com
Printed in the USA
LVOW11s1150101113

360580LV00001B/8/P